I Am Because of You

Brother David Steindl-Rast
Translated by Peter Dahm Robertson

Paulist Press
New York / Mahwah, NJ

First published in German as *Ich bin durch Dich so ich* © Vier-Türme GmbH, Verlag, Münsterschwarzach 2016.

English translation copyright © 2017 by Paulist Press, Inc. Translated by Peter Dahm Robertson.

Library of Congress Control Number: 2017937018

ISBN 978-0-8091-5359-6 (paperback)
ISBN 978-1-58768-725-9 (e-book)

Published by Paulist Press
997 Macarthur Boulevard
Mahwah, New Jersey 07430

www.paulistpress.com

Printed and bound in the
United States of America

8245

CONTENTS

PREFACE

First, a disclaimer: this book contains much that is autobiographical, but it is not actually an autobiography. For each of the nine decades of my life, I have chosen a characteristic theme and written down related memories. The nine interviews then go deeper into the respective themes. I realize that such a framework has advantages and disadvantages. One of the advantages I see is that it excludes details that spring only from the talkativeness of an old man and only serve curiosity. One of the disadvantages is that not all themes that were important to me fit within the framework. I was especially sorry that I could not include the dialogue between science and religion in which I have repeatedly had the privilege of participating. As a Lindisfarne Fellow since the 1970s, as speaker at the Cortona weeks of the ETH Zürich and the Waldzell Meetings of the Stift Melk, and as a participant in the Mind and Life Fellows Program, I have had the opportunity of meeting important pioneers of the sciences. My life has been additionally enriched by my friendships with Joachim Bauer, Fritjof Capra, Stanislav Grof, Amory Lovins, Pier Luigi Luisi, Reinhard Nesper, Herbert Pietschmann, Rupert Sheldrake, Tania Singer, and Richard Tarnas. To all these encounters, I owe my conviction that science and religion are two inseparable attempts to orient ourselves in the inner and outer realms of this one reality. They belong together.

I also regret that I can mention the names of only a few friends throughout the text. But here I do want to express my

I Am Because of You

thanks personally to those whose help made this book possible: I was able to work on it in silent isolation on the S'Alqueria estate of Stephan and Viktoria Schmidheiny; Brigitte Kwizda-Gredler was my first reader and gave empathetic advice; Johannes Kaup insightfully held the interviews; Diego Ortiz Mugica added new photographs and improved old ones; Alberto Rizzo and Julian Fraiese were of equal help; Brother Linus Eibicht, OSB, (publisher) and Marlene Fritsch of the Vier-Türme-Verlag awaited, shepherded, and published the German edition with great patience. The prayers of many friends and the encounters with many people whom I will never know by name encouraged me and strengthened me in my writing, finally bringing the book into the hands of its readers. I am grateful to all of you.

I want to dedicate this book to my brothers—my two biological brothers, Hans and Max, and their entire families, as well as my Brothers, the Benedictine monks of Mount Saviour, New Camaldoli, and the Gut Aich monastery in St. Gilgen; there especially, Father Johannes Pausch, since I wrote it only out of love for him and following his wish.

—Br. David Steindl-Rast, OSB
Mount Saviour Monastery,
August 6, 2016

INTERVIEWER'S ACKNOWLEDGMENT

This book has an unusual style. It is divided into nine decades that sketch out the processes of learning and maturing in Brother David's life. The memories of each decade, written by Brother David himself, precede the nine interviews ("dialogues"). These dialogues attempt to explore his life and thinking as well as open new horizons of questions building on his reminiscences. Through the reflective writing, on the one hand, and the collected but also lively and spontaneous dialogue, on the other, two different narrative forms have emerged. They may not seem stylistically unified, but they have the advantage of a resonant questioning and answering to the author's rich legacy. They also lead to a critical and self-reflective view on what has passed and what is to come in Brother David's life.

"I am through you so I"—with this deep line of E. E. Cummings, David Steindl-Rast summarizes his ninety years of life. And the many layers of this "through you"—with you, in you, because of you—reaches from his birth to beyond death and grows tangible in his writing. It can get under one's skin and reach one's heart—at least, that was my experience when I first visited Brother David in the mid-nineties in the southwest United States, and had the honor of speaking to him face-to-face. Then as now, we were separated by forty years, but during an encounter with him, that is as irrelevant as so much else. He is concerned with the Now, which transcends the flowing passage of time, bringing the present, the past, and the future into its full richness.

Brother David adamantly refuses to be set on the pedestal of the master. But he remains unquestionably a spiritual master, though he has never founded or wanted to found a school. He has students all over the world, and they have less learned a specific method from him than they have been inspired and fascinated by his heart's wisdom, which comes out of the genuine monastic tradition, by his attitude of deep listening and farseeing, and by the gratitude that arises from these. Anyone looking for the esoteric in Brother David—a gnostic secret knowledge that is imparted only to the wise and enlightened—will be quickly disappointed. No, for him everything begins with creation itself, with the everyday, which to him can become a question about the foundations and entirety of our being. For that reason, doing the dishes—his regular chore in the monastery—is no less a spiritual activity than theological consideration of the Holy Trinity.

Brother David is convinced that all people face the Mystery of life. Everyone, no matter their origins, education, culture, or religion, knows the Mystery, even if many ways of access to it have been cut off by corrupt or broken off traditions. Steindl-Rast is concerned with getting the wellspring(s) of faith to flow again, to make its power fruitful for shaping life, and to work toward greater justice in the world, firmly and spiritually grounded in the Mystery.

Even in his ninety-first year of life, one can still see how Brother David, who has already discovered so much, returns to being a searching novice. This tangible beginner's mind, his multi-faceted curiosity, and his sheer childlike joys attract many. He is also a living example that one can be old in years without losing any of one's mental freshness. It is possible that this is made easier when one does not need to "make" oneself but can receive every day anew: I am because of you.

Interviewer's Acknowledgment

Thanks for this book is due to many people, not least Brother David himself; Brother Linus Eibicht, OSB, the publisher of the Vier-Türme-Verlag for initiating the project; and prior Johannes Pausch, OSB, for his regular and patiently encouraging help in the production of the book. Additional heartfelt thanks go to Marlene Fritsch and Brigitte Kwizda-Gredler. Both spent long nights proofreading the text versions of our dialogues with watchful eyes, and giving advice along the way. Silvia Tschugg contributed constructive criticism and practical help with formatting. We are also grateful to Argentinian photographer Diego Ortiz Mugica and Alberto Rizzo for making that connection; and likewise, Matthias Gahr. Most of all, I want to thank the monks of the Gut Aich monastery. They continually received me with open arms and hearts when I arrived for the dialogues in this book. Without them, this book could not have become what it is today, and what it will hopefully remain for all readers: a document of living and considered gratitude.

—Johannes Kaup
Vienna, September 1, 2016

1

BECOMING HUMAN

FINDING MY HEART'S CENTER

1926–1936

Adam in the Garden of Eden—this memory, gilded with myth, of the beginnings of human history is mirrored in what is probably my earliest memory: I am still small enough to look up at the underside of a tall tulip.[1] I can see only its underside, but I want to look inside the blossom, so my father lifts me into his arms and lets me look into the flower from above. A bitter smell rises from the tulip, its interior shining darkly with soft stamens.

We are encircled by flowers; white gravel paths lead to little ponds above which ancient linden and chestnut trees stretch out their branches: my personal Garden of Eden.[2] A high wall—which for me was the quintessence of feeling protected—surrounds the rambling park of this coffeehouse my father has inherited in the suburbs of Vienna.

My parents, my two younger brothers,[3] our "Detta,"[4] and I live in one of the side wings of this little palace from the time of Empress Maria Theresa. The central wing, meanwhile, with its large ballroom and several smaller rooms, belongs to the coffeehouse.

I Am Because of You

A stone spiral staircase leads up to the second floor, which I call "the old floor" because my grandmother and great-grandmother live there. The "old floor" is my favorite place. It is where my grandmother builds me a tent using a colorful tablecloth, spread over the backs of two armchairs. In that space, I experience the feeling of belonging and being protected, and it is there that my grandmother brings me snacks and drinks. Together, we marvel at the beautiful dance of dust when sunshine streams into the room between the two curtains. We also pray together. My grandmother introduces me to the Lord's Prayer, the Angelus prayer, and soon the entire Rosary.

At this stage of my life, distinct and distant realms of reality are still joined together completely in my mind. It is prior to Christmas, everything is shining with joyous anticipation. There is something glinting on the carpet in my parents' bedroom. I take up the tiny piece of gold thread between my thumb and forefinger. What can it be? "Perhaps the Christ Child has come by already and lost a hair from his locks?" my mother suggests. That is enough to transfix me. In retrospect, too, I should say, for me, that was a true, albeit childlike, encounter with the unfathomable Mystery with which all of us as humans must engage.

On another occasion, I look up through the trees and see something like a tiny white dove in the cloudless blue sky. Wings outstretched, it glides through the air silently and leaves a trail of huge, cloud-like letters: *I M I.*[5] I ask Detta what this might be, and without much interest, she answers, "That's the skywriter." I shiver with a deep reverence. For years, I did not share this experience with anyone, for adults seemed suspect to me if they could be so indifferent to something so sacred: the skywriter! That must mean the Holy Spirit! (I would never have imagined that the letters were an advertisement for detergent.)

This is also the time when I dreamt of an image that—without knowing at the time—would become fundamental to my understanding of my life.[6] In the dream, I am walking down the stone spiral staircase of the "old floor." Halfway along the stairs, I am met by Jesus Christ, who is walking up from the floor below. He looks just like the picture that hangs above my grandmother's bed. We move toward one another, but instead of walking past each other, we melt into one.

The myth of paradise includes the fall of man and the expulsion from the garden. I had only just entered the second grade of my Catholic elementary school on the *Rosenhügel* (Hill of Roses) when my parents' divorce completely changed our life. In retrospect, I can see how young they were: my mother was only eighteen when I was born. Our coffeehouse, not far from Schönbrunn Palace, was a popular location with Viennese on day trips. Hundreds of guests came on sunny weekends, and our supply of pastry was taxed to the limits; when it rained, all the expensively purchased baked goods went to waste. To this was added the depression of the early 1930s. Each week brought agitation and disappointment, an external strain that certainly contributed to the failure of my parents' marriage. From then on, my father was gone. We three boys lived with my mother in the vacation home my parents had built in Prein on the Rax in the Eastern Alps. In the alpine valleys of the time, life often resembled the Middle Ages more than anything else. More has changed there in the last eight decades than in the preceding centuries. There I experienced Christianity—the amalgamation of culture and Christian tradition, the unquestioned acceptance (albeit not complete living) of Christian values.

The holy days of the Church calendar and the local traditions gave the year a fixed structure: for Advent, we children would set up the model of the manger and would open a new window of the Advent calendar each day. Christmastime, with its miracles that returned every year and were newly miraculous again each year, officially began on Christmas Eve, when my grandmother served her fish soup, which we found revolting but of which she was so proud. Then there were the prayers beneath the Christmas tree, which seemed to us children to drag on endlessly before we could look at our presents; family visits on St. Stephen's Day; communion wine on the Feast of St. John, Apostle and Evangelist; the Austrian tradition of molybdomancy on New Year's Eve;[7] star singing on Epiphany; and blessing the candles on the day of the Presentation of the Lord. After the high spirits of carnival, we received an ash cross on our foreheads on Ash Wednesday and imposed small sacrifices on ourselves during the time of Lent. Long before Palm Sunday, we would begin searching eagerly for the most beautiful branches for our palm bundles, and then it was Holy Week already, with all its rich traditions: the unpopular spinach soup on Maundy Thursday, our shy kissing of the cross on Good Friday, the visit to the cenotaph of Jesus, and—in those days on Holy Saturday—the celebration of the resurrection, accompanied by the ringing of the bells, which had "flown away" and been silent since the Gloria on Maundy Thursday. The Easter eggs and Easter ham were blessed after High Mass on Easter Sunday. Soon thereafter, we put up the maypole. Taking it down was no less celebrated, as were the St. John's Fires up in the mountains for the summer solstice. Our name days—celebrated even more than our birthdays—also framed the progression of the year; as did the saints' days, particularly the assumption and all other holy days related to Mary. These "holy times" were like dances for us children.

There were only two classes in the Edlach elementary school: our teacher Miss Riegler (*die Riegler Fräul'n*, as she was known in the local dialect) taught the first three grades, while strict Schoolmaster Straßmaier instructed the fourth through eighth grades. Before school, the girls would dance under two linden trees in the schoolyard or play jump rope and hopscotch, and we boys had our own games, such as tug-of-war. While soccer was not permitted in the schoolyard, it was intensely followed all the same. After all, at the time, the Austrian "Wunderteam" had even beaten the English team. We listened to cup matches over the radio, and to this day I remember the name of our hero, Sindelar, even though spectator sports never interested me again. Sometimes in winter, we were allowed to ski to school and, on the way back, could hitch ourselves to the horse-drawn sleigh with which our baker, the *Schindlerbäck*, delivered bread and rolls.

I became an altar boy and had to memorize the prayers of the Mass in Latin. To get to the Rorate masses in Advent, I had to trudge through the deep snow before break of dawn. Altar boys in the parish church of Prein were even allowed to operate the bellows for the organ, but the little Monastery Church of the Merciful Sisters, on the edge of the workers' settlement in Edlach, had only the harmonium on which Sister Viola would accompany the singing on Sundays. Back at home after the Sunday Mass, we would often play "mass" again. Our friend, Geyer Karli, was always the priest and seemed, in our eyes, to be able to repeat the sermon word for word. Our young chaplain, Father Franz Rudolf Kopf—fresh out of the seminary—also preached well. He had a Puch motorcycle and would sometimes take me with him up to the Preiner Gscheid Pass in the mountains to watch the night sky and learn the names of the constellations. He supported my mother—who did not remarry—and remained a fatherly friend to my brothers and me throughout our later life.

Soon, my two brothers and I were allowed to participate in the star singing on Epiphany. Each of us wanted to be the Black King, so the honor was determined by chance: our mother had baked her ring—showing St. George as dragon-slayer riding his horse—into a special Epiphany cake, and the brother whose piece contained the ring was allowed to blacken his face with soot and don the most beautiful of the paper crowns. Then, draped in linen sheets and bearing our homemade star, we set out to our neighbors' houses.

It was also a tradition for us boys to bring the newly blessed Easter fire home with us from church on Holy Saturday, so that the kitchen stove could be freshly lit with its flames. We had long

I Am Because of You

before made containers from empty tin cans which we would swing on strings to fan the embers of the bracket fungus we used as coal. It was important to know where exactly we had to make the holes in the old cans. Our older playmates dutifully taught us these arts, just as the games and counting-out rhymes of the schoolyard were passed on, step for step and word for word, from the older to the younger children. It was not so easy to whittle a hazel twig into a whistle that actually did whistle loudly; or, when tending the goats, to stoke the fire in such a way as to achieve the perfect temperature for roasting jacket potatoes; or—particularly tricky—to fashion a wooden fork into a reliable slingshot. Zens Ferdl was especially skilled in this regard. I can still see Ferdl shooting a swallow off the telegraph wires before my very eyes. It was dead, but still warm. I felt complicit and would have cried from guilt, but boys don't cry!

Swallows' nests were too high up in the cowshed, and the nests of the redstarts high on the gables of our roof were unreachable. But in the beech wood forest behind our house, there was a birds' nest one could peer into. Only after I had given my solemn promise never to go there alone, Sommer Hansl showed me the secret place. How artfully the nest had been woven! A single egg lay in it. Despite my promise, I snuck back on my own, but not just to look; I had to touch this egg. And suddenly, the yoke was all over my fingers. To my promise were added my lie that it hadn't been me, along with all my pangs of remorse. Paradise was lost to me not just through my parents' divorce—a disgrace in those days, and something that I could not speak of to anyone even late into my adult life—but through my own guilt as well.

But near the end of the first decade of my life, I was given the gift of the very experience that would give me inner strength after my loss of paradise. The childlike dreamer had become a little rascal. I was rarely ill, thank God. And if we children ever did fall ill, our beloved *Herr Doktor Bittner* called at our house at any hour of the day or night. He would diagnose us as soon as he walked in, simply by the smell of the sickroom, and make us healthy again. That was how easy it was.

There I was sitting in Dr. Bittner's waiting room with my mother—I have since forgotten my ailment at the time—and was starting to get impatient. I have already thoroughly observed the leeches in their glass, and—as inconspicuously as possible—have studied the goiter of the woman sitting across from us. My impatience was once more demonstrating what I have so often been reproved for: having "mercury for a behind." But my mother does not say that this time. Instead, she lays her hand on the part in my hair and says, very quietly because of the other waiting patients, "Try to do what people in Russia do: they can sit completely still for hours, just breathing in and out and holding Jesus' name in their hearts with each breath." (That was my first encounter with the Jesus prayer. Why my mother ascribed it to the Russians, specifically, I do not know to this day; perhaps she had read *The Way of the Pilgrim*. But her advice that day gifted me the Prayer of the Heart.) I close my eyes, breathe calmly, and think on Jesus. Everything else happens by itself: I discover my heart as a silent inner space where I am at home with Jesus. I begin to realize that I can come home to this center whenever I want. From then on, this insight gave my life an anchor I cannot lose. It is this homecoming that gives the image of melting into one with Christ—the relatively static image I know from my dream—its dynamism.

DIALOGUE

JK: Brother David, your earliest biographical recollections reveal that, even as a child, you were filled with an unquenchable curiosity, a joy in discovery. Your world was a place where you experienced deep connections, and this feeling of connectedness seems to come from your wonder in the miraculous. On the one hand it is wonder at nature, on the other hand your prayers with your grandmother probably gave you an early inkling of something intangible, something larger, greater than what is immediately around us—the gold thread, for example, which you described finding just before Christmas. In retrospect, you interpret such moments as an initial meeting with a Mystery beyond understanding. Additionally, all of that was embedded in a still unbroken relationship with the Christian faith. What sort of a spiritual world was it that you were born into?

DSR: In retrospect, such wonder is truly important, central even. One could say that wonder is oriented in two directions: one is amazement at and appreciation for the beautiful; the other is reflection on it. Reflecting is more than just thinking. It means opening oneself to the things that are worth wondering over. This is the sense in which Plato means that philosophy begins with wonder,[8] and both orientations have been important to me throughout my life: on the one hand, admiring and praising the beautiful, and on the other hand, wondering about something mysterious that extends beyond it.

JK: That requires some sort of resonating chamber, in your family, for instance. That's why I ask: What kind of a world was it that you were born into, for it to be possible for you to interpret those moments in such a way? That isn't an inevitable attitude.

DSR: What enabled me to take that position was a feeling of being protected. It is quite astounding that my parents and my grandmother made it possible for me to feel so protected. Because I was born only eight years after the end of the First World War, it was certainly not inevitable. It was a time of total societal collapse. And yet I grew up in this little "pre-war" world where I felt I belonged and was protected, while outside the long garden wall of the park on which I grew up, parades and rallies were being held, and screaming and commotion could often be heard. I can remember it very vividly.

JK: Were these parades and rallies already connected with the rise of the National Socialists?

DSR: I am sure that this movement was already starting back then, yes. And anything was possible. The early 1930s were almost a time of civil war. I remember how once as a child I walked out through the large garden gate. There were flags and screaming and I scrabbled back and forth between many legs. But then I was found and brought back. So, that feeling of protection is probably the most important and fundamental feeling that made it possible for me to grow up in a sense of wonder.

JK: You were four or five years old when you had this remarkable dream where you encounter Jesus on the staircase, and as you pass one another, the two of you melt into one. This amalgamation with the Holy was foundational to you and has influenced your sense of life in the following years. Even early on, Jesus seems to have been a fascinating figure for you. Looking back, how do you make sense of that?

DSR: In fact, I find that inexplicable. But I believe that all people are oriented toward this enormous Mystery. We are conscious of the fact that we stand before what we cannot grasp. Most of all, it was probably my grandmother who led me to the things that mentally come together in my dream image of Jesus. Jesus and God—for me there was no real difference at the time. I believe that as a child, I saw Jesus as a collective image of the entire Divine Mystery.

JK: But in your dream, you melt into one with the Divine Mystery, so with its real image, the real presence.

DSR: And that, I believe, is a lesson that this Mystery itself gave me from the beginning. I cannot imagine that that is something that a child would invent. And thinking was not even a part of it. It is a gift of life, and it has always stayed with me.

I Am Because of You

JK: What does that tell you today?

DSR: At the very end of my biographical reflections, I write of the double realm. This double realm is something I grew into very early, and it has stayed with me throughout my entire life. Furthermore, it is becoming more and more tangible. The danger that my thinking and feeling would break apart was never very great to me. On reflection, that too was a great gift. As far as I can remember, what I felt and what I thought never came into conflict.

JK: Meaning that one stimulated the other. Or to put it differently: One could hardly think without being in some way emotionally directed, but one is often just unaware of the fact. When you feel, that influences your thinking.

DSR: And if you continue this line of thought, that means that the beautiful and the good were inseparable to me. As Theodor Haecker said, "The beautiful feels itself in feeling, and the good wills itself in willing."[9] In other words, the beautiful, the good, and the true should not be apart. The true recognizes itself in recognizing, the good wills itself in willing, and the beautiful feels itself in feeling. For me, that has always been a single thing from the beginning. I had to gradually separate it, analyze it to distinguish its parts. But sometimes it seems to me that, for other people, the beautiful and the good are not one in their eyes from the beginning. To them, they start out separately and must be brought together gradually. My development happened somewhat differently.

JK: You seem to have had parents and grandparents who encouraged your joy in discovering the world and lay the cornerstone of a confident, creative personality in you. I know several people in whom this joy for life was halted or disappointed early, or gradually poisoned. Reflecting on your early childhood, what are you most grateful to the people around you for?

DSR: For me, the most important thing seems to be a trust in life. I received this gift of trust in two ways: First, all the people close to me proved themselves to be trustworthy. They were simply there for me, the small child, when I needed them. Without question. My mother was not always physically present, even if I would have liked that. I remember it very well: When she put me to bed, I would say, "Stay here, stay here! Why do you have to go?" She would always answer, "I need to earn *kreutzers*." She had to work in the coffeehouse in the evenings—but she was trustworthy. And second, I was trusted, which was just as important, if completely different. I was sometimes astounded at what I could do without being supervised or checked on.

JK: What sorts of things?

DSR: For example, how we played. Even as small children, my brothers and I were allowed to go into the woods alone for hours, walk up the creek, and explore. At the time, I think that my mother knew more or less where we were and that we were in no danger. We felt protected, on the one hand, because we somehow knew that she was taking care of us. But on the other hand, she gave us that trust, so that we were free. Later we would go exploring for weeks at a time, and she did not know where we were, because at the time, there was no way to call and let her know. She gave us this gift of trust anyway, confident that we would take care of each other, and that we would give each other trust and prove trustworthy. Those two aspects are what I am most grateful for.

JK: As children, we feel protected and free until we have an experience of fear—fear that we may lose something familiar. Fear for our own existence. I imagine that, for you, the early divorce of your parents must have been one of those breaks. In that way, the economic and political depression of the 1930s had its parallel in private unhappiness. How did you personally experience your father's departure?

I Am Because of You

DSR: My mother and younger brother were gone suddenly. I was the only one who was already in school and thus stayed in Vienna with my father, who was very kind to me and tried hard to care for me. But taking care of a child and running the business at the same time was simply too much for him. So, he sent me to the boarding school on the *Rosenhügel*, where I was already enrolled as an external pupil. Of course, for such a young child as I was, a boarding school was dreadful, but I was only there for a short time. Then my mother came one night and took me with her. The separation from my father was not really painful, but I think I may simply have suppressed that pain. I always prayed that my parents would get back together. I remember that very well, but I did not consciously experience any pain of separation from my father, so I probably suppressed it.

JK: In the later years of your youth, were there any situations where you wished for a father?

DSR: No, not really. In retrospect, I feel that my mother, as far as possible, also filled the father role well. I cannot remember yearning, wishing, or searching for a father. In my early youth, just after the war—I would have been around eighteen or nineteen years old—we rediscovered our father with our mother's help, and then had a very good relationship with him all his life. The relationship with a father that is formed in the early years of childhood is missing.

JK: But not painfully, as you say?

DSR: It was not painful at all. I can compare that with my mother: when I was separated from her for even three days, I missed her a great deal. But I cannot remember ever missing my father as a small child. Not in the least. But that might also be repression.

JK: Was he less present than your mother in the family system even before the divorce?

DSR: He was very present, but he was also very strict. He was a very loving father, but when I was a small child, he was very strict about things such as eating everything on your plate. His absence, therefore, may have been freeing, in a way.

JK: Your childhood during your time in the country between Schneeberg and Rax is couched in the rhythm of the seasons, the rhythm of the holidays and traditions of the region. As an altar boy, you were connected to the local version of the Christian tradition. But then there is also that scene, reminiscent of Mark Twain, in which you refer to yourself as a rascal, with "mercury for a behind," who not only breaks a promise but then lies about it. I'm referring to the story of the birds' nest. Psychologically, that is quite easy to understand, because one wants to preserve the integrity one is projecting outward. But you felt guilty and interpreted the story as akin to the fall from grace. Seen from the outside, that feeling is no more than a peccadillo; seen from the inside, however, it is more. How did you experience guilt at the time? And were there forms of reparation?

DSR: Guilt was connected closely to the Ten Commandments: it was very clear what one was or was not allowed to do. If I did something one was not allowed to do, I felt guilty. I did not question that. The reparation was to go to confession. I felt that as unpleasant, but then again also as very freeing. I had difficulty asking for forgiveness.

JK: How did you experience your guilt? What were you afraid of if you had to live with that guilt?

DSR: I had no fear of hellfire or anything similar.

JK: Psychologically speaking, could you have lived with that guilt at the time? It may have been little guilt, but you were also very conscientious.

I Am Because of You

DSR: I was always conscientious, but that was not due to ideas such as eternal damnation. From the beginning, I was certainly religious enough to conclude that God is gracious; that is the most important facet and that is why everything will be alright somehow. I still remember that my mother must have felt that I did not rise on my hind legs and defend myself enough. A boy who was a bit older than I was, Löschl Loisl, was often quite rough with me, and at one point, my mother saw that and said, "Go on and defend yourself!" So, I jumped at him and hit him, and he immediately had a nosebleed. But that was horrible for me. I felt so sorry for him. It was an important experience for me.

JK: That you felt sorry for him or that you could defend yourself?

DSR: No, that I felt sorry for him. I did not really doubt that I could defend myself if I wanted, but I really did not want to, because I did not want to harm others. That became very clear when I actually did harm him.

JK: There is this scene in which you are becoming impatient during a doctor's visit with your mother. It resolves very unexpectedly. In this situation, you, as a fidgeter, are introduced to the Prayer of the Heart by your mother, without knowing that it has a long tradition in Eastern Christianity. In retrospect, you describe this as one of the first turning points in which your experience of melting into Christ now calls up a complementary, dynamic experience. How do you understand this dynamic experience? What was new in this religious dimension?

DSR: As I have already said: Jesus and God. *Jesus* was simply a keyword for God and the Divine Mystery. The new aspect was that I, whenever I wanted, could have access to this Mystery in my own heart. Through the Jesus Prayer, I could go to that center of my heart and feel protected in Jesus. That is what this experience amounts to in the end. That was something new and lasting, it is true.

JK: But it is astonishing that you had this experience so early. I imagine it made complete sense to you only later, in the time when you were a monk. Was it something you felt intuitively?

DSR: I believe it made sense to me from the very beginning, and over the course of my life, I have learned to understand and practice it better and better. But it made sense to me immediately. It was like a sudden enlightenment.

JK: You said that this is where a dynamic impulse is added from the experience of amalgamation in your dream. How do you conceive of these two sides, melting and dynamic?

DSR: What is dynamic is that I myself can actively go to this place. My dream was simply an experience that stayed in my memory. I was not even aware that it influenced me. With the Jesus Prayer, something entirely new started, which is the dynamism: there is a presence of God within me which I can approach and to which I can return over and over again.

JK: In what kinds of situations do you feel urged or drawn to pray the Jesus Prayer, to return, as you say?

DSR: Probably whenever the outside situation becomes difficult. Of course, in that context, I remember the dramatic experiences of bombing and war and all the things that were truly externally threatening. But my own short temper has also gotten me into trouble again and again. Essentially, anger has been the main point of friction with my environment.

JK: Where did your anger come from?

DSR: My mother always said, "Just like your father." My father was also very short-tempered. I probably inherited that.

JK: Can you remember any situations in which your temper got the better of you?

DSR: Of course! For example, we had huge oak armchairs that came from my ancestors' old home. I once picked one up and threw it to the ground, so that it split in two.

JK: Can you still remember why?

DSR: I have no idea. The smallest causes made me angry in such a way.

JK: Which made the Jesus Prayer something saving.

DSR: Yes. It is of course also possible that this anger was repeatedly caused by repressed pain, such as over my parents' divorce.

JK: So, things return....One significant Catholic intellectual movement with which you came into contact early on was what was known as the liturgical movement in the 1920s, centering around the theologian and Augustinian choirmaster Pius Parsch.[10] Parsch had advocated making the Bible and the liturgy comprehensible and immediately understandable for the people. Against the initial opposition of his superiors, who continued to advocate the Latin liturgy, Father Pius Parsch, almost forty years before the Second Vatican Council, did something then unheard of: he held congregational masses in the church of St. Gertrud where parts of the Tridentine Mass were sung by the congregation in German. That won recognition at the *Katholikentag* in 1933, where a so-called *Singmesse* was first held. What is astonishing is that at the age of seven, you participated at that very gathering in Vienna, holding your grandmother's hand. How much of that can you remember?

DSR: The only thing I can remember is the microphone, because my grandmother showed it to me explicitly: "Look, that's the Cardinal speaking into a microphone. That way we can all hear him much better." And this thing consisted of a large ring, with the actual microphone suspended in the middle of it on long springs. That image is very clear in my mind. Nothing else—no people, no flags, nothing. But later, as adolescents during the war, we would walk on foot to St. Gertrud's to hear Pius Parsch. First, you had to walk through Kahlenbergerdorf down to Nussdorf. Then, up along the Danube all the way to Klosterneuburg. That was a lovely long way. And on some Sundays, we walked that way to go to the masses of Pius Parsch.

JK: Were you impressed by that at the time?

DSR: Very, but in my school, we were already celebrating the Mass turned toward the people, likely influenced by Pius Parsch.

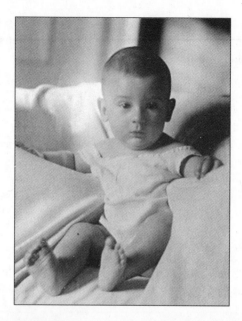

In the arms of my grandmother

2

BECOMING CHRISTLIKE

BETWEEN HUMAN DIGNITY AND HUMILIATION

1936–1946

The things we remember, but also the things we forget, say a great deal about how we see ourselves. I know, however, that what my memory selects from my lived experience, and the structure and order I give the memories when relating them, depend on inextricably tangled connections. Nevertheless, I feel justified in singling out from the first decade of my life my dream of melting into Jesus Christ and my encounter with the Prayer of the Heart. They laid the groundwork and paved the way for my later experience. After all, in the dream, I found the dawn of a conception of myself that would deepen in each subsequent stage of my life—and that deepening continues even today.

What seems significant about the Prayer of the Heart is that to the more static conception of who I am inside, the Prayer adds the dynamic component of being able to come home to Christ. Only because I know that I can always return to my center again, am I able to face what confronts me in the second decade of my life. To begin with, there is the departure from my home, which is painful. I am sent to a secondary school, which in my case, was a boarding school. Though the *Neulandschule*[1] gives me all that my heart, open as it is to wonder and joy, could wish for, I feel terrible homesickness when, after a weekend at home in the country, I sit on the evening train back to Vienna. Only returning to the home in the center of my heart can help me with that pain, and so I gradually learn to live in the Prayer of the Heart.

That is the only way to endure the blows that will rock my young life again and again: the *Umbruch*, "upheaval," occurs, and my brothers and I are suddenly *Mischlinge*, "mixed breeds." My grandmother cannot return home from America; her sister disappears in a concentration camp. Systematically, the Nazis destroy the spirit of our beloved *Neulandschule*. I am drafted into the German Wehrmacht, where, especially in the military, the Jesus Prayer allows me access to a hidden inner world in which I can continue to live my true life; I am often hardly aware of the things going on "outside." Even when being bombed, and during the chaos at the end of the war, I can always return to the interior of my heart, where—in the poetic words of Werner Bergengruen—"there is nothing that may frighten you, and you are at home."[2]

Again, there are two experiences that allow me to understand my memories of these years in terms of their inner structure—two diametrically opposed experiences. The first epitomizes our lives as *Neulandschule* students and summarizes the most important things for which I am grateful to this school. Without any sanctimonious displays of pietism, the chapel service was unquestionably the heart of our school life. Even then—a lifetime before the Second Vatican Council—the altar faced the congregation. There were no church furnishings. We stood during the mass—the boys typically with their legs spread wide—and knelt on the bare floor. Much of the liturgy of the mass was read in German and prayed by both congregation and priest. One of the prayers during the preparation of the Eucharist kept calling itself to my attention. It began with the words, "God, You created Man wonderfully in his dignity, and even more wonderfully renewed him."

Dignity was a word that I had quite possibly never encountered in everyday speech before. That might be the reason why it especially impressed me; but I slowly grew to realize that human dignity was at the center of the important concerns: becoming a Christian, our education, and also our entire life. The very fact that we were permitted to address our teachers and educators by their first names gave us dignity—us as much as them, since "Mr. Teacher" is nothing more than a title, and a family name does not convey the personal as directly as a given name. Dignity and appreciation lie within personal encounters. We were gifted that experience by the *Neulandschule*.

It would be hard to find a more harshly opposing approach to personal relationships and appreciation than in the German military. I am grateful to the *Neulandschule* for my awareness of what being a Christian means. In the barracks of the Krems Pioneer Corps, I learned what the opposite looks like. Everything here was structured to exterminate any consciousness of human dignity. We were not trained to murder people but rather "the enemy." Each of us was nothing but a tiny, easily replaceable part of a completely impersonal, fine-tuned war machine. Any self-confidence was systematically taken down. For example, as recruits, we had to take part in classes to learn the composition of each branch of the German army and its specific functions. Following a short lecture by the sergeant, we were given an oral test: "What are the parts of the German army?" It made sense to answer, "The German army is divided into the following parts...." At the word *divided*, the sergeant immediately flew into a rage, screaming, "The German army is not *divided*!" And the punishment was immediately given: "Squat on your locker and scream, 'I am an ugly little dwarf,' eighty-six times!" The metal lockers for our uniforms reached almost to the ceiling, and whoever had to squeeze into the scant space in between soon really did feel like

23

an ugly dwarf. The number 86, meanwhile, was the number of our Pioneer division. (Often, we wished for a lower division number.)

All the experiences in this second decade of my life can be slotted into the broad spectrum between dignity and humiliation, and have some connection to one or the other of these two opposing poles. I experienced the spirit of the *Bund Neuland* for barely two years. In that time, I became acutely aware—admittedly more intuitively than intellectually—that being a Christian was linked to the appreciation of human dignity.

Then Hitler came. We heard on the radio how thousands in the streets cheered the invading German troops. My Jewish relatives sat weeping in the half-darkness of their apartment near Maria am Gestade, their curtains drawn. I would never see most of them again. Soon, the shop windows of Jewish businesses lay in shards. Those who refused to participate in the boycott were denounced publicly: "This Aryan swine buys from Jews!" My mother was considered only a "*half*-Jew," and therefore did not have to wear a yellow star. But during Sunday Mass, I stood not far from a woman who was wearing one. Voices were soon raised: "Get out, you! There's no room for Jews here!" She hesitated for only a moment; then she was gone. I wanted to run after her and say something comforting, but what? And already I had missed my chance—I am still ashamed of that.

Hitler's reign in Austria coincided precisely with my teenage years, so my typically teenage rebellion against authority found its obvious release in resistance to Nazi propaganda. But my rebellion was also clearly articulated in the ideal of being Christlike. We would probably have simply said, "*Our Führer* is Christ." Admittedly, one could not say any such thing if one valued one's life, but we sang, "When all become disloyal, *we* shall remain true," and knew secretly what we meant by those words. We also sang the German folksong, "*Die Gedanken sind frei*" (Thoughts are free) with fervor.[3] Many of our friends from the *Neulandschule* sang that song as loudly as they could when they were arrested and driven away in police vans after attending a concert of the Don Cossack Choir. The Secret Police knew that "resistant" youths would sing Russian songs in protest and always attended the Choir's concerts in droves. After one of those concerts, conducted by Serge Jaroff, my brothers and I were fortunate to escape. Approximately two hundred others, among them our friends Bernhard and Georg von Stillfried, were interrogated by the Gestapo on the Elisabethpromenade for two days before being given an official warning and then released. Over a dozen of those questioned, however, were never seen again.

The contempt for human dignity found its most gruesome form in the slaughter of youths on the front lines. Continually, the youth masses we celebrated half-illegally with Father Arnold Dolezal turned into masses for the dead to honor our recently fallen friends. And how passionate friendships are when one is so young! But time and again, a friend would be drafted into the military and be dead soon thereafter. No one could escape military service.

Then I was called up myself. My drafting orders on May 31, 1944, felt like a death sentence. I could not know that, as if by a miracle of countless acts of providence, I was to spend eight months in the barracks, instead of being posted to the front, and that I would then be able to go into hiding at home in Vienna. Even during those dark days in the barracks, a light of humanity keeps shining through in my memory, brilliant and unforgettable. Once again, as the rest of my division was sent to the front, I stayed behind because I had been assigned to a training unit. The entire unit came from the same area: they were Black Sea Germans, whose ancestors had emigrated down the Danube on disposable ships known as *Ulmer Schachteln*, or "Boxes from Ulm." These young men spoke German as one might have heard it in Vienna over a hundred years earlier. Hitler had brought them back, put their wives and children in a camp somewhere, and drafted the men into the Wehrmacht. The dignity of these people, the regard with which they encountered one another, will always remain in my memory. With what tenderness, almost shyness, they spoke of their women and children when the lights had been turned out in the sleeping hall, and with what deep sadness! After the weeks of our Pioneer training, they were sent to the front, while I, once again, stayed at home. Apparently, their transport train mistakenly drove into a train station occupied by Russian forces. Although they each counted themselves as Russian citizens, they are believed to have all been shot on sight.

The end of the war in a city destroyed by bombs, lacking water and electricity, and without food was, admittedly, even more chaotic than the years of the war. For hours we stood with our pails, lining up to use one or another of the few water wells that still existed in the neighborhood. Our main source of food was saltbush, a kind of weed that grew on and in the rubble of bombed houses.

But amid this chaos, our chaplain, Father Alois Geiger, gave a shining sign of human dignity. Each day, punctual to the minute, he would wander over the mounds of rubble from destroyed homes and offer us survivors holy communion. There were also relationships that developed with many of the Russian soldiers. For example, the first wave of occupying troops consisted of friendly young men who supplied us with bread and soup, and there were even some who spoke German. One of them had a wounded hand, and my mother made him a dressing with her "miracle ointment." He came back to our home every day to get the bandage replaced. Once, he was very drunk, and while bandaging his hand, my mother appealed earnestly to his conscience. The next day he refused to come into the house, but called from the street and stuck his hand through the garden gate for the bandage to be changed.

The second wave of occupiers turned out to be far less friendly. Day and night one could hear women calling for help. Many were raped. Several times, my mother escaped as if by a miracle, and later fled to a convent in the 15th District. The Russian soldiers were also after a Ukrainian forced laborer, Nadja, who had worked in the neighboring house but had flown from them. They threatened to shoot me if I did not "send Nadja out" immediately. Our neighbor, who had heard the threat, tried to help. They let me go and shot him instead. "No one has greater love than this, to lay down one's life for one's friends" (John 15:13). I am conscious every day of the fact that I owe Viktor Springer my life.

In early summer of 1945, amidst all this turmoil, the word began to spread that Cardinal Innitzer was calling on students to help the Sudeten-German refugees who, exiled from newly founded Czechoslovakia, were streaming into the *Marchfeld* by the thousands. We donned priest's robes, because that granted us at least some respect from the Russian soldiers, and set out without the slightest training, instructions, or medication. Compassion and awe for the suffering of the displaced were all we brought with us. All we could do was set up refugee camps in parishes and empty schools and try to ensure the greatest possible hygiene in toilets and the water supply. Here, too, regard and appreciation of their dignity amid their misery proved to be the most important, perhaps the only things we could give these poor people. Today, in the face of new waves of refugees in Austria, this memory seems relevant again.

At the end of the second decade of my life, the image of the tulip from my childhood memory reappears. This time it is the ten thousand tulips that Wilhelmina, queen of the Netherlands, gave the city of Vienna as a gift after the war. In Vienna, they bloomed in all their glory in even the smallest park, where handwritten signs—"3 Russian and 5 German soldiers. Names unknown"—still mark mass graves. Nothing could have given these humiliated people of the city a renewed consciousness of their dignity more impressively than this truly royal gift.

DIALOGUE

JK: According to the Greek philosopher Parmenides, faith begins as a deep trust in being. To me, your years of youth seem to have been accompanied by this deep trust, which then takes shape in a specific religious practice. As an adolescent, you learned how to be a Christian, or rather, how to become Christlike, as you have said. Your school years fell directly in the era of a fresh start in Catholicism, the *Neuland* movement. You attended the *Neuland-schule* in Grinzing in Vienna, founded in 1926. The late 1930s, in which the German Anschluss of Austria also took place, was a humiliating time, a time that deprived people of their dignity. Meanwhile, human dignity that grew out of a Christian spirit was the lived spiritual environment at the *Neulandschule*. How did that place influence you at the time?

DSR: When I think back, the most important and decisive gift the *Neulandschule* gave me was the joy of life, expressed in a completely new way as a kind of independence. That probably also includes being personally appreciated in dignity. As students, we were taken seriously, we felt honored. Today, when I pray the verse *spiritu principalis confirma me* from Psalm 51,[4] that reminds me of the spirit of a young prince, and every time that makes me think of the *Neulandschule*. In the first two years of school, that is, in the time in which the spirit of the *Bund Neuland* still permeated the school, I really did feel like a young prince.

JK: What effect did that have?

DSR: Joy in life and complete trust that everything would work out—and a spirit of adventure is obviously part of that as well. The phase of a young hero going out into the world was one that I experienced very clearly and at a very early age, between ten and twelve. That was also the time during which we went on excursions, another experience of independence.

JK: Clearly, there were some teachers who understood themselves as companions for life, as mentors and promoters.

DSR: Many of them I can remember well, especially my teacher during those two years, Friedl Menschhorn, whom I feared—he was quite strict—but who also taught me much that inspired me. Then Dr. Franz Seyr, who was my German professor, also became a dear friend to me and my family. We had the good fortune that, when the Nazis invaded, he did not need to flee and could energetically continue communicating the spirit of *Neuland* during that time.

JK: He wasn't replaced by someone loyal to the party?

DSR: Dr. Seyr was not the director, but our class leader. He helped me again and again—politically as well. At one point, he advocated strongly for me when I was in trouble. I had significant problems with the Nazi leadership of the school. The best thing he could do was to write on my report card, "A positive attitude toward national socialist schooling would seem desirable." I still have it. This formulation alone was extremely dangerous. But he ensured that nothing worse stood in its place, which was a way of supporting me in this aspect. He also helped me a great deal by introducing me to the writing of Martin Buber and Ferdinand Ebner.[5] He himself was later the editor of Ebner's collected works.

JK: Ebner was a personal-dialogical philosopher who worked as an elementary school teacher in Gablitz near Vienna, but also one of the twentieth century's most important thinkers. Unfortunately, and unjustly, he is less well-known than Buber.

DSR: Several of the things that Martin Buber was to write in *I and Thou,* Ferdinand Ebner had already published two years earlier in *The Word and the Spiritual Realities*. Throughout his entire life, Buber felt somewhat ashamed. He knew that Ebner had published certain insights almost verbatim, a little earlier than Buber himself had.

I Am Because of You

JK: Did the two know each other personally?

DSR: I do not believe so.

JK: At the time, life under Nazi rule meant that people had to show their colors. You and your friends from the *Neulandschule* lived in spiritual resistance against the *Gröfaz*, the "greatest general of all time."[6] When you say that your counterimage was Christ as *Führer*, you are referring to a spiritual leader who himself can do nothing against the power and violence and terror of Nazi rule. At the same time, he must have been a powerful source of motivation for the resistance. How did faith help you at the time, in the face of brutalization, persecution, and violence? What enabled you to stay upright and even advocate for others?

DSR: The poems of Reinhold Schneider helped us a great deal.[7] We often sent out a newsletter to our friends in the military, and those would frequently contain poems by Reinhold Schneider, and of course a great deal of Rilke and several things we had written ourselves. Our hero, our leader Christ did not seem powerless to us at all. I can only speak for myself here, but what I pictured was that at some point, all this terror will be over and Christ reigns eternal.

JK: At the same time, one did see that the powers of this world were almost omnipresent and that to many, resistance against them seemed almost hopeless. Early on, what one believed in probably had little power against the things happening politically, on the battlefields, or in the concentration camps.

DSR: We did not think in those terms. There was no question that the power belonged to God and to Christ. We never doubted that. However powerful the others might play themselves up to be, it might be a difficult and very unpleasant situation, but it always remained on a completely different level.

JK: This situation was not merely unpleasant, but deadly at times.

DSR: It was a dreadful reality, but we were able to laugh about it. There was this joke: "The first volume is called *My Struggle*; what will the second one be called?...*My Paintings of the Island*," which implies sending Hitler, the former painter, to an island like Napoleon before him. The comparison between Napoleon and Hitler seemed appropriate. We thought that it won't be long, and he'll be gone again. That was how one thought of it, even early on. Horror and comedy need to be seen alongside each other. On the one hand, the comedy: from the very beginning, we were constantly making fun of the Eternal Reich, the Thousand-Year-Reich. That it could be both ridiculous and deadly, deadly in the full sense of the word, for more of my friends than survived it—as it might have been for me by a hair's breadth—these two things somehow stand close together.

JK: Adolf Hitler, the great demagogue and nation seducer of the twentieth century, privately admired, as Friedrich Heer has shown, the historical power of the Catholic Church.[8] Though he had contempt for the Church and for clerics, and subjected them to bloody persecution, *My Struggle* actually contains a theological justification for his project of destruction, the Holocaust, when he says, "Thus did I now believe that I must act in the sense of the Almighty Creator: by defending myself against the Jews I am doing the Lord's work."[9] Hitler was not a theologian, and his thinking was certainly influenced by atheism, but he conceived of and legitimized his political actions in theological terms. The ideas of providence and destiny are another example. Consequently, he was able to tap into a religious language and symbolism that his adherents at least knew from cultural memory. Looking at the party conventions in Nuremberg, one can understand how well the Nazis knew to hijack religious rituals politically and reinterpret them with the goal of making people subservient. Why, in your opinion, was it possible for so many people to succumb to this fascination, to this "political religion," as Eric Voegelin has described it?[10]

DSR: Put succinctly, they were blinded. The way I understand it, Hitler, Himmler, and all these other great evildoers were blinded. Today, we present it as if Hitler had known exactly how bad his actions were, but that he cast them in a kinder light and performed them anyway. I cannot put myself in his frame of mind, but I believe that it is closer to reality to say that he was completely blinded. He truly believed that he was acting justly, for example, by exterminating the Jews.

JK: One always acts under the impression that one is doing the right thing, *sub specie boni*.[11] But Hitler had announced his intention to destroy the Jews. The idea is presented and could be read in the book *My Struggle*.

DSR: Until the end, Hitler believed that he was doing something good by doing what he did. There is something tragic in this belief; it shows the dangers of ideology and answers also why so many people fell for it. They were equally confused and let themselves be blinded by it.

JK: It is possible, perhaps, to explain confusion and blindness. But the question then becomes whether I start killing other human beings in the name of blindness and confusion.

DSR: That is precisely what the confusion consists of: to believe that one can or even is compelled to commit injustices against others because it is God's will or the "right thing" to do. Unfortunately, that belief still exists today.

JK: The danger isn't over?

DSR: While we exclude anyone from the circle of belonging, we are sinning. In other words, we are tearing the fabric of the world and of humanity. We are making a tear in it. Only when our feeling of belonging encompasses everything can we speak of love. Love is a lived yes to mutual belonging. It does not need to be the emotion of loving someone. Today, that is becoming relevant again regarding the question of refugees.

JK: Where specifically do you see that relevance?

DSR: In the question, Do we belong together, or are those people "others"?

JK: Today, though, people who are afraid ask themselves different questions. Some might think that maybe we do belong together on some higher level, but there are still too many in my immediate surroundings.

DSR: In practice, of course, those are very difficult questions. But if you truly say, "We belong together on a higher level," we need to ask ourselves how we, together, can find a solution to our problems on the lower level. How will we manage that? The point is not that others are a problem for us and we need to think about how to solve it. No, we all share a problem. How can we solve it together? One always needs to set out from the perspective of togetherness.

JK: Let's return to the topic of national socialism, to the fascination that emanated from Hitler and his movement of a fresh start. Was there tense discussion within your extended family?

DSR: There were no differences of opinion about it. But, of course, that was also caused by the fact that many family members with whom we lived were Jewish. There was no question at the time. My brothers and I were considered "quarter-Jews" as well. We did not talk about it much, but we were aware of the danger we were in.

JK: That description is based on the Nuremberg Laws regarding race. Did you feel Jewish in any sense based on cultural or religious belonging?

DSR: No, but we were close to our Jewish relatives who had to flee. My favorite aunt, my grandmother's sister, died in Auschwitz.

JK: So, to return to the topic, there were no discussions in your extended family that...

DSR: ...that there might be something good in it?

JK: Or that some would have taken that position out of opportunism, as was the case in some families. Some might have said, "Well, then we'll just need to come to some arrangement," or, "it's not so bad, let's wait and see," or, "finally we can get work," or whatever other arguments were brought forward.

DSR: No, there was nothing like that in the part of the family I knew. After the divorce, we stayed with my mother's family, and there was no debate about that, if only because my mother was a "half-Jew."

JK: If your mother, according to the Nuremberg Laws, was half-Jewish and her sisters and close relatives were deported to extermination camps, then would your greatest fear not have been for your mother? And, vice versa, did your mother not have the greater fear for you and your brothers, since as spiritual resisters, you were always in danger of being detected and persecuted by the Nazis?

DSR: It is one thing to recognize the danger and another to feel that fear in real life. I would call it caution rather than fear. We just had to be cautious. One knew whom one could trust, and we even knew spies who had infiltrated the youth movement. Someone had shown us pictures of them and warned us. I can still remember it clearly. Near the end of the 38 line,[12] someone showed me a man who tried again and again to infiltrate the movement. We were careful, but I cannot say that we lived in constant fear. Instead, we lived in the conviction that the situation is terrible but would pass. At one point, my mother was ill in her bed, and a Gestapo officer came and asked her with whom her children fraternized. She was prepared and mentioned people who really were our friends, such as Klaus and Lopi Brehm, the children of the writer Bruno Brehm, who was popular with the Nazis.[13] Because my mother looked Aryan, the Gestapo officer believed that she was the one who had the Aryan heritage in her marriage. He even said to her, "It is a real shame that you married a Jew. That is just like crossing a thoroughbred horse with an ass." Afterward, all my mother said was, "If I had not been so ill, I would have jumped out of bed and strangled him."

JK: She seems to have been a brave woman, your mother.

DSR: We called her the lion mother. When the war was over and the German soldiers were fleeing from the Russians, the front lines were passing through our house. One night, two wounded German soldiers came into our house and asked, "Aren't there any men here who could bring us to the German lines?" My mother was keeping me and a friend hidden, so to get the men out of the house quickly, she said, "There are no men here, but I will lead you!" Then, in her bathrobe and in the middle of the night, she led the two soldiers through the vineyards back to the German troops. She then ran back quickly to be home again before the Russians came after the Germans. She was also a serious mountain climber and had already been up the Matterhorn. At the time, it was not such a tourist attraction as it is today. We would look up the cliff faces and say, "Look, mother was up there." We would never have dared to attempt those difficult climbs.

JK: At the time, the Catholic Church was certainly under immense pressure, even if, from today's point of view, one would have wished for more courage for resistance. How did you experience that time in which minds differed so radically, in which true Christian faith had to stand its ground in the face of a racist-populist ideology of salvation?

DSR: I experienced that only in small ways, in our own situation. At the time, we asked our spiritual companion, Father Dolezal, "Can we kill Hitler?" It was the old question of tyrannicide. His answer was, "Yes, if you can get at him." The chances of that were slim.

JK: This circle around Father Dolezal, the so-called Do-Circle, was an important nest of spiritual resistance and also central to your religious education?

DSR: The Do-Circle was the most important aspect of both religious education and resistance in those days. Dolezal himself hid one of us, Alfons Stummer, in a small room behind a closet in the rectory of St. John of Nepomuk in the Praterstraße for two years. Alfons was a deserter. We knew nothing of this. No one did back then. Father Dolezal was a very brave man. In fact, he was the main figure giving us strength and stability. The Do-Circle was incredibly important to us. We celebrated masses weekly and held discussion groups. That was our real source of strength.

JK: How big was this circle?

DSR: It got smaller and smaller because more of us kept getting drafted. But there were also many girls who were part of it. I would say it was about twenty to thirty people.

JK: During these war years, Christian ideas were one prong of resistance, but you also read a great deal of Rainer Maria Rilke in your circle of friends and in the Do-Circle: Rilke's *Book of Hours* and his story "The Lay of the Love and Death of Cornet Christoph

Rilke." Why this highly aestheticized literature in the face of death and destruction?

DSR: That very fact may have been considered a retreat, of which such a resistance is often accused, in retrospect, for not being aggressive enough, for pulling back. We did also read Trakl: "Mankind marched up before fiery jaws,"[14] I remember it well. But what somehow did give us stability and comfort was the *Book of Hours*. The story of the Cornet was more inherited from the youth movement and belonged to the Nazis as much as to us. The youth movement only began to split slowly in the mid-1930s. One group placed the religious aspects more in the center; *Neuland* was part of that. The others were slowly subsumed by the Hitler Youth. But our roots were the same, and there were still a great many positive things that remained, even under Hitler. It is not fashionable to say that these days, but there were positive values as well.

JK: Such as?

DSR: Such as connectedness with nature, the joy in the natural, joy in the simple life. Wiechert's *The Simple Life* was a book that we read a great deal in those days.[15] I do not believe that it was advanced as a disguise of true aims. The people who were lured to the wrong path ideologically looked primarily to these positive values and accepted all the other aspects. Those who were not lured looked at the same positives but did not accept the negative aspects. That was the real difference.

JK: To return to Rilke, what was fascinating, what gave strength in these days of depression? What was so fascinating for you about the *Book of Hours*?

DSR: These poems were prayers in a language that appealed to us a great deal. They were so completely different from the liturgical prayers, and we could make them our own more easily. Praying was of central importance to us in those days. One of Reinhold Schneider's poems begins with these words: "Only the praying may yet succeed in staying the sword above our heads." Here was a deeply central thought. Georg Thurmair was important to us as well.[16] The calendars in the youth houses always contained several of his verses appropriate to the pictures.

JK: In an earlier conversation, you described the war years in which so many of your friends and companions lost their lives due to bomb strikes in Vienna as "years of the utmost aliveness." How should that be understood, given the fact that you could have despaired and fallen into resignation at each stroke of fate? Where did the defiant sense of life and life-affirming courage come from?

DSR: I think that many people today experience the same thing when they encounter mortal dangers: aliveness flares up even more. For me, the reason seems to be that one is forced to live completely in the present. The degree of our aliveness is measured in the degree to which we do not cling to the past or look to the future but are truly in the *Now*. In those years, we were forced to do that, and that is why we were so alive and joyful, despite everything else.

JK: Because you were looking death in the face?

DSR: Because death was constantly before our eyes, we were forced to fully enjoy those possibly last moments of our lives.

JK: So, live each day as if it were your last.

DSR: In that sense, yes.

JK: You do not know whether you will wake up tomorrow.

DSR: As children, we had to go to the air raid shelter practically every night during the war years.

JK: During one of those raids, you did not make it into the shelter.

DSR: That was in our house in the Kaasgraben. Our landlord had built his own air raid shelter, and since he had no children, we were allowed to flee there as well. One time, we were unable to close the heavy door because the pressure from the falling bombs was so strong and kept pulling it back open. This was during the time when we were already having to lay our clothes in the evenings, so that we would be able to find and put them on quickly even in the dark; one was not allowed to make much light. In Vienna, the turning out of lights had been ordered. During air raids at night, we would have to find and put on everything quickly and then go to the shelter. Even today, I still set out everything I take off so that I can find it in the dark. It has become a habit.

JK: After the end of the war, the Russian occupation followed, which you have described as ambivalent in that the first wave of occupying soldiers was liberating, while the second was more oppressive. As we know today, there were systematic rapes of tens of thousands of women by occupying forces. I was very touched by the scene in which you described wanting to pro-tect Nadja, a Ukrainian forced laborer from your neighborhood, and how a neighbor came to your aid. This neighbor paid for his moral courage with his life. Did you feel at the time that your last hour had come—or rather, that by an act of providence you had escaped with your life?

DSR: I was in a state of complete shock. I did not even think of that aspect. But I should clarify, we were not protecting Nadja. We did not know where she was. She had gone. She simply fled. One could not say that I was not afraid; I was simply in shock.

JK: Then why was your neighbor shot?

DSR: The Russian soldiers were probably drunk. They wanted to find this girl and could not, so they threatened to shoot someone if she did not appear. They let us go; our neighbor was at hand. But he was not the only one. They let some ten or twenty people march all the way to the church, where they were stood against a wall. The soldiers shot wildly. In the end, one of them was dead. They may not have intended that at all. The others were hurt. Viktor Springer lived in the house next to ours, and the Springers had a forced laborer too, from Poland, named Sophie. She saw me in uniform many times, and when the Russians asked her, "Is he not a soldier as well?" she said, "No, no, he is just a child." By doing that, she saved my life.

JK: As did Viktor Springer.

DSR: Yes. I think of him as having saved my life. When the soldiers were menacing us in the other house, he came to the garden gate and shook it. They heard the noise, let us go, ran down, and shot him.

JK: So, to clarify the situation, the two Russian soldiers were looking for Nadja but came into your house and questioned you, if one can call it that.

DSR: I suppose I must have been standing somewhere close by. It all happened in the street, in this broad suburban road with no traffic. Then the soldiers led me not into the house in which we lived but to the second floor of a villa on the opposite side of the street where a resistance fighter who had been an officer in the First World War lived. He was probably too old to be drafted by then. He was active in the resistance and very brave. In this moment, he kept talking at the soldiers who had put their machine guns to our heads. His wife was standing there as well. They had put a bucket over her head. He kept talking to the Russians—in German—and I suppose it is difficult to shoot at someone who keeps talking to you. And in the meantime, Viktor

Springer was rattling the gate downstairs. So, they turned, left us standing there, and we were then free.

JK: That saved your life. In all the turmoil after the end of the war, with millions of refugees, you and your friends followed Cardinal Innitzer's call to assist the Sudeten-German refugees.[17] You write that you had no specific training and no knowledge: "Compassion and awe for the suffering of the displaced were all we brought with us." What reaction did these actions cause in you?

DSR: It was yet another kind of encounter with great human suffering.

JK: Some of the Sudeten-Germans even came on foot.

DSR: All of them came on foot. Some of them pulled little carts onto which they had packed all their possessions. That may also have been the first time I had to give practical care to truly poor people. There was hardly anything we could do. We saw to it that they were housed in relatively humane conditions and had clean water and toilets that were at least reasonably hygienic to prevent cholera and dysentery.

JK: What encounters can you recall from that experience?

DSR: I can remember children, for example, who had bloody knuckles from knocking at doors begging. Seeing that, we organized little groups to go stealing cherries. There was no one who could have harvested them anyway. One evening, several children arrived on a cart and said, "Mother is lying back there on the street and having a baby." We had nothing but a bicycle, on which we went to look for her—and found her. The child had not yet come, thank God. We then led her back to the camp slowly, where she had the child.

JK: That is truly an incredibly exciting time, to swing back and forth between life and death and experience all the emotions.

DSR: It was certainly formative, but we only attended to what needed to be done, moment by moment. There was no time at all to think about it. This needs to be done, this is how help needs to be given now. We did not think of anything more. We never would have considered thinking about how terrible it all was.

JK: So, you might say that it was a completely human impulse, which you were then able to see in a larger interpretive framework of faith.

DSR: It was nice that we could do this work within the framework of the Church. As Catholic youth, we were in the heart of the places where it was happening. The only help we could always count on were the priests. They made the schools available to us and used the pulpit to ask for things we needed. Many priests hid and even defended women from the Russians in their parishes.

JK: Defended in what way?

DSR: At one point, we came to a village where a pastor had hidden about forty women in the parish rectory. A Russian soldier broke into the house, but the pastor grabbed him and carried him out. He wanted to drown him in a small stream, at which point the soldier bit off his thumb. So, we were greeted by a pastor with only one thumb.

JK: Did he actually drown him in the end?

DSR: No, the Russian soldier ran away.

JK: And never returned?

DSR: No, he was never seen again.

JK: Quite the stories...

DSR: Of course, in the end, we did all get diarrhea. Many of the refugees as well, I'm sure. Following that, I had to return to Vienna.

3

DECISION

1946–1956

My wonder knows no bounds—the war is over and I am still alive! It dawns on me slowly at first; then, suddenly, I can see the truth with my own eyes: a whole life is before me! I am simultaneously overjoyed and frightened by this insight—frightened because I sense that this is as great a gift as it is a responsibility. What should I make of my life? Seizing any one of the countless opportunities before me means letting go of all the others. What is most important to me? Looking forward, I think about this question and feel that *what* I do will be less important to me than doing whatever I do with joy. And looking back at the years of war, I see that especially in the darkest, most unhappy moments, that inner joy I am concerned with gave me strength—it is a joy that does not depend on happiness or unhappiness. But on what does it depend? I brood over this question. And then, out of the blue, a sentence comes to me: "To have death before one's eyes at all times." Yes, really, "out of the blue"—out of the most joyous blue sky. It is a bright August day in Salzburg. I have been invited here by friends, among them an enchanting girl with whom I am in love. The city is filled with music; everywhere, summer breezes carry tunes across streets and squares, down promenades and through open windows. This is the first year that the Salzburg Festival is once again being held in a free Austria. In exchange for a packet of American cigarettes, an usher casually discovers two free orchestra seats and we can hear and see Mozart's *Don Giovanni*.

The end of the opera recalls the sentence to my mind: "To have death before one's eyes at all times." The sentence remains in my head. It is from the *Rule of St. Benedict*, a short book that is almost fifteen hundred years old. I had read it as a student because, to spite the authoritarian regime, we would read anything that displeased the government. These few words, of all things, made an impression, and now it begins to dawn on me why: these past years, we young people have had death before our eyes, so close we could touch it. It now seems that more of my friends died on the front lines than were left after the war. And at home, too, bombs had brought daily destruction and death. A single incautiously whispered word could result in the death penalty; one of our chaplains was arrested and executed.[1] But despite all that, in retrospect I must say that for me and my friends, those terrible years of war were also years of true joy, a joy I wish never to lose. Hence the question, On what did this joy depend until so recently? Now I have the surprising answer: we lived with such joy because we were forced to have death before our eyes at all times. That forced us to live in the moment— completely in the *Now*—and that was the secret to our living joy.

So as not to lose this spark of joyous aliveness, in the future I will therefore need to "hold death before my eyes at all times" as well. I had found this guiding thought in the *Rule of St. Bene- dict*. Did that mean that I would need to become a Benedictine monk? At the time, this thought made me queasy, and so I pre- ferred to go dancing. No one dances the polka with as much fire as my Elisabeth. The two of us live on the *Festspielstiege*, and each morning I walk down to St. Peter's Archabbey, where the

I Am Because of You

Benedictine monks have mass. In my Schott missal I can follow along with the Latin mass texts for the day in German. Every day, it seems that the reading, yet again, concerns decisions; I am captivated by the topic, even if only half-consciously. Hesitantly, I consider whether the joy that is so important to me might even be worth becoming a monk for. I am divided against myself, but shrink back from making a decision. The next morning, the first reading in the mass tells of the famous judgment of Solomon in 1 Kings 3: two women bring one child before the king, and each claims the child is hers. Solomon has a sword brought and says, "Cut the child in two and give each woman half." One of the women cries out, "No, give *her* the child!" thus proving herself to be the true mother.[2]

In that moment, something in me cries out as well, and even then, the judgment of Solomon has caused in me a long-ing for inner wholeness that will not let me go. It is illogical, but I now know that becoming a monk will be my path, however far the detours may lead me.

I will run from the consequences of this decision for the next seven years, finding one alibi after the next: studies at the Academy of Fine Arts, a diploma as an art restorer, cofounding a successful children's magazine,[3] working as a restorer, journeying to the United States, studying anthropology, travels as the prefect of the Vienna Boys' Choir, a year in Florida, doctoral studies in psychology at the University of Vienna....

In truth, I had been unknowingly prepared for the experi-ence of my "calling." After the end of the war, my brothers and I renewed contact with our father. He was now living in East Tirol and got me a job as a farmhand over the summer holidays. Hard work and hearty farmers' meals sound seductive—but on the sec-ond day, I am sent straight up to the mountain pastures, known as the Alm, where food is less plentiful. All the same, the solitude and silence, surrounded by the peaks of the Dolomite mountains, become an experience of deep contemplation and inner joy.

Decision

The only other people up on the Kerschbaumer Alm are "uncle" and "aunt"—distant relatives of the Kerschbaumer farmer for whom I am working—who have lost their homes in the war. We live primarily off *Sterz*[4]: Aunt cooks, Uncle and I sit across from one another, and Aunt puts the pot between us. On the first evening, we both start at our edge and work our way toward the center, but Uncle is quicker and works his way past the middle into my territory. From then on, I start by making a line down the middle of the pot and eating from the center toward me. That way, we get along. I learn to milk and otherwise handle sheep and young cattle. I can walk across the Alm for hours, listening to the silence and reading my pocket Bible—particularly the psalms, which I read over and over. But I also read the Song of Songs, the other Wisdom Writings, and the stories about King David, who also began his life as a shepherd.

I remember a moment from the first year after the war that casts light on the circuitous path from my beatific experience on the Alm to my similar later experience as a novice: A few friends and I are standing in a crowded tramcar on the 38 line. We are talking about our plans for the future; the others seem to have clear-cut career paths in mind. Something in me resists such clarity. "I'd like to encounter many different things before I make my decision," I hear myself saying, and listen, astonished, as I spontaneously use a metaphor to express my idea: "The broader the base, the higher the pyramid."

So, to expand the "base of the pyramid," I study at the Academy of Fine Arts, where I passed the entrance exam during the war. And since I am interested in primitivism and children's art, I also study ethnology and developmental psychology at the university. Bombs have destroyed the university buildings, so the first thing we students must do is help with the reconstruction. We do so with the joy of new beginnings and rebuilding. After we have completed the mandated hours of shoveling rubble—marked in our student passes—we are permitted to enroll in a course of study. In the summer of 1947, I visit the United States for the first time. Even the crossing, which I complete on the SS Marine Falcon, a small troop transport ship, is an adventure. I have been invited to a meeting of Christian students in Chicago. I still remember how our Austrian delegation was supposed to sing Austrian folk songs, but how all of us began to cry so much from homesickness that we could not keep singing. From Chicago, American students give me and my friend, Isabel, a ride to California. From there, we return to New York by bus, which takes an entire week. Then we board a ship of the Holland American Line back to Europe. (At the time, flying across the Atlantic was financially out of the reach of mere mortals.)

My second journey to the States is initially planned as a visit to my grandmother, and to my two brothers studying in New York—but a surprise extends the trip. While I am in New York, I receive a telegram from the Vienna Boys' Choir stating that one of the prefects has been denied an entry visa at the last minute. Could I accompany the Choir on their North American tour in his stead? The invitation came because, as a student in Hinterbichl, the Tirolean summer home of the Choir, I had worked as a prefect, which meant that their rector, Monsignor Joseph Schnitt, knew me. And so, for over three months, I ride across the United States on the Choir bus, together with the boys, my colleague Paul Grande, and Choir director Peter Lacovich. We have two concerts every three days and, including brief visits to Mexico and Canada, cover more than two hundred miles a day. It is very taxing for the children. I have nothing to do with their musical education, but must instead ensure their physical and mental well-being. One of the boys, Werner Scholz, who later worked as an engineer and for years served as the head of the St. Pölten branch of the charity, Caritas, will remain my lifelong friend.

One of the things from the Vienna Boys' Choir tour that was to become most important to my life was my encounter with an American choir, the Apollo Boys' Choir of Palm Beach, Florida.

Decision

Their founder and director, Coleman Cooper, invited me to work as a prefect in his choir after the Vienna Boys' Choir had returned to Austria. The prospect of living in Florida was tempting—but what came as a surprise was that I would be living in an extraordinarily beautiful palazzo, imaginatively decorated in the style of the Italian renaissance. In the early 1920s, Philadelphia art patron Joseph E. Widener had commissioned architect Maurice Fatio to create *Il Palmetto*, embedding half a dozen original reliefs by Luca della Robbia in its walls. Now this paradise was the home base of our American boys' choir. The attendant park extended across the entire strip of land between Lake Worth and the sea. Throughout my life, I have often had the privilege of calling particularly beautiful places home. None of them was more beautiful than this palace, where "Mama Cooper," as the boys called her, cared for them and me as a mother would. It was an additional piece of good fortune that I was allowed access to the choir's recording equipment, as I was working on my dissertation about vocal expressiveness at the time. In those days, recording devices were extremely expensive, and their operation was nowhere near as simple as it is today. The magnetic tapes kept jumping off the reels, or they would tear and have to be spliced, and sometimes I was entangled in them from head to toe, like Laocoön and the snakes. When I had finally collected the necessary material, I returned to Vienna, wrote my dissertation, and attained my doctorate in psychology in November of 1952 under Professor Hubert Rohrbacher. Fortunately, I was able to return to New York City for Christmas that year to celebrate and be with my family. That winter journey across the storm-tossed Atlantic would be my last crossing on a steamship. Only many years later would I return to Europe—that time by airplane.

My immigration to the United States—not the sort of place one usually comes to become a monk—was my third time in the country and soon became a time of crisis for me; that time, after all, I had not merely come for a visit. True, I was happy to be with my family, but city life in Manhattan was not for me. The only place I truly felt at home was the huge, dimly lit, silently vaulted reading room of the Public Library on Forty-Second Street. I spent countless joyful hours there, and even today I am still grateful that I had the chance to do so.

One of my cousins was a psychiatrist in New Jersey, and I worked for him, helping treat mentally ill children. A former colleague from the Vienna Academy of Fine Arts already had a prominent position at the Philadelphia College of Art, and I received work from him as well. But my heart was not in it. I did not know where it belonged.

My culture shock in the "New World" lead to days of depression; what began as an attempt to escape gradually turned into the question of whether the right monastery might not be waiting for me somewhere after all—even in the United States. Unexpectedly, the question would arise and, in a single moment, give me the certainty that I had arrived. I said to a friend, "If I had lived in the Middle Ages, I might have become a Benedictine monk, but there is too much tradition weighing down the monasteries in Europe. What I'm looking for"—yes, I heard myself saying that I was looking for something—"is a monastery as envisioned in the original Rule." "That's strange!" my friend answered. "Apparently that kind of reformed monastery was just founded near Elmira in New York State." I immediately called the Greyhound Bus company, found a night bus to Elmira, arrived there the next morning, and after some searching, discovered the farm on which three monks had founded the monastery community of Mount Saviour.[5] That afternoon, I worked with one of them, Father Placid. We planted pumpkins, and he answered my questions satisfactorily. The next morning, I returned to New York with two other guests. That was in mid-May of 1953. I asked to be accepted into the monastery, and on August 20, I finally arrived at Mount Saviour to stay. Suddenly, the decision had become easy. In my first years at the monastery—as postulant, as novice, and then as a young monk—I felt quite like I had on the Kerschbaumer Alm. The third decade of my life ended in the rolling hills of the Iroquois much as it had begun high in the Alps. As I did then, today I still listen deeply each day into the silence and space.

DIALOGUE

JK: The art of living well is also the art of dying well—*ars vivendi est ars moriendi*. You had already read the *Rule of St. Benedict* during the war, and in the face of the daily possibility of death, you got to know central spiritual principles. When people speak of religion today, many think of ways of life that are controlled from outside, marked by rules and commandments. For those people, religion is problematic, irrational, a potential source of conflict. Only few associate spirituality with being alive, wakeful, and living fully. But this aliveness and all its possibilities were available to you, Brother David, in a freed Austria after the end of the war. You not only have death constantly before your eyes, but a whole bouquet of options. Which were the ones that attracted you most, initially?

DSR: At first, I wanted to continue what I had already begun when I was drafted: my studies at the Vienna Academy of Fine Arts. Professor Karl Sterrer, whom I loved and admired a great deal, had been caught in the political wheels. He was made a scapegoat, even though he was no Nazi but had only joined the party to protect himself and others. At any rate, he was then so disappointed that he either left or was unable to teach at the Academy anymore. After that, I never found another painting teacher who fit me well, so instead, I studied art restoring with Professor Eigenberger. That was fascinating. After the war, as restorers we received a great many destroyed objects.

JK: What sorts of places did you do your restoring work?

I Am Because of You

DSR: With a few exceptions, we always worked in the Academy's studio, for example, on a painting by Lucas Cranach, the paint of which had bubbled during a fire—I think it was the fire in St. Stephen's Cathedral. We had to use a great deal of care and effort in repairing that painting. There was also a work by Albrecht Dürer: a Madonna belonging to the Austrian state, which was then apparently traded to the Stifter Museum in the (now Czech) city of Oberplan. Another thing that was very exciting for us students was that every day from noon to 1:00 p.m., the professor would offer free expertise to people who wanted a valuation of their real or supposed art treasures. We could watch every day, too. Most of the time the things weren't very valuable; pictures generally turned out to be copies. But once, someone brought in a folded canvas, and our professor immediately said, "That could be something interesting. We need to take a closer look at it." It was impossible to see the picture clearly, since it was very dark and extremely dirty. After weeks of work, it turned out to be a previously unknown Van Dyck. We were the first to discover it. There really were some very interesting results. But what touched me most during this time was a lecture by Professor Koppers on the origins of the idea of God.[6]

JK: He was a theologian?

DSR: No, he was an anthropologist, but he was a priest of the Steyler missionaries. At the time, they represented a number of professors of the anthropology department. Yes, I was very moved by this lecture. I went to the Austrian National Library afterward and borrowed the various volumes of Wilhelm Schmidt's *The Origins of the Idea of God*.[7] I sat in the Café Bastei on the Schottenring, and wept as I read. Following that, I studied anthropology.

JK: Can you remember what it was about the book that moved you to tears? Was there a special idea or realization that stirred you?

Decision

DSR: Wilhelm Schmidt's *Kulturkreis* theory is largely obsolete today. But what remains and what really touched me at the time was that the God Idea is a shared primeval human experience. That is what Father Wilhelm Schmidt's volumes illuminated for me.

JK: That there has always been a kind of primeval religiousness or faith with all peoples—is that what you mean?

DSR: He articulated it quite differently then, but that thought continued in my mind. Today, I can see that what makes us human is that we grapple with this great Mystery that we can cautiously call God. This idea shone on me like a light in that moment, and that moved me so greatly.

JK: So, you studied anthropology. You describe the summer of 1946 as free and magical. If I interpret it correctly, you as a then twenty-year-old were in love with a girl named Elisabeth. You wrote that she was an excellent dancer and that you not only visited the Salzburg Festival with her but also did quite a bit of dancing yourself. If you were in love, then were you considering marrying and founding a family?

DSR: No, I did not consider it so much as plan it. I pictured it in detail: I wanted to have twelve children. But then, I kept remembering that overpopulation is growing, and that thought really did have a very serious influence on my decision to live a celibate life.

JK: You thought that you didn't want to bring more children into the world because there were already too many? But that was back in 1945, when the world population was only two billion people.

DSR: Since then, humanity has tripled in size. That is completely unimaginable.

JK: When you're in love, you don't necessarily think of overpopulation.

I Am Because of You

DSR: Today, young people do not even necessarily think of a family and children. But at the time, we did think of that. It was part of our frame of reference.

JK: For both of you?

DSR: In our entire generation's frame of reference, love, marriage, and family still belonged together, that is what I mean.

JK: So, you pictured it for yourself. And on Elisabeth's side?

DSR: I do not know. But I believe that picturing was rather one-sided.

JK: Your love as well?

DSR: Largely.

JK: At any rate, nothing more came of that on the relationship level. But at the time, you didn't yet know that you wanted to live alone, did you?

DSR: Since my experience in St. Peter's Archabbey in Salzburg, I did know, somewhere deep down, that was my path: becoming a monk.

JK: You are referring to the scene where, as part of a service in St. Peter's, you hear the Bible text on the judgment of Solomon—a child is to be split with swords, and the true mother saves the child by giving it up. You relate this text to your own life: you did not want to live feeling torn in two. But why did you relate it to yourself at all? In what ways did this wholeness take shape for you?

DSR: At that time, I had this "either-or" in my head constantly and felt the dangers of inner division. I became aware that we had always been whole, undivided. That is why we were so happy even during the war. We had to live in the moment because death was always before our eyes. I then connected the experience of "keeping death before your eyes at all times" with being a monk, because I had read the sentence in the *Rule of St. Benedict*. I realized that, as a monk, my life would become whole; I would live in the moment and be happy. So, I wanted to become a monk, but at the same time, I didn't want to.

JK: So, at the same time, twelve children would have been an attractive option as well, were it not for overpopulation?

DSR: Very attractive, and many other things were as well. At the time, I pictured being a monk as something quite grim. I was still undecided in this "either-or."

JK: Had you read Søren Kierkegaard at the time, his book *Either/Or*?

DSR: We did read Kierkegaard during the war, but I do not think that had any influence on my decision. Apparently at a reception, a woman enthusiastically thanked Kierkegaard for his book *Either/Or*. I was the same way. I wanted both: either *and* or. But the judgment of Solomon made me reflect.

JK: So, you are saying that at age twenty, you realized that you wanted to live in wholeness. And yet it took several more years for you to start living that "both one and the other."

DSR: Precisely. Often in life, an insight appears long before it is finally put into practice or even before there is any will to put it into practice. I lived this either *and* or and was unwilling to decide, despite being simultaneously able to see that I did not want to live a divided life. I could see this particularly clearly after the Bible reading of the judgment of Solomon.

JK: Can you remember why it was particularly this passage that spoke to you and gave you such clarity?

I Am Because of You

DSR: The imagery is very clear: to me, the two women were, on the one hand, the Church, the true mother; and on the other, the world, both claiming "that child is mine!" The true mother relinquishes her child to keep it alive—but in the end, the judgment of Solomon restores it to her. That image did not let me go, I was simply constantly pushing it away from my conscious mind.

JK: ...and went on to completely different studies. The broader the base, the higher the pyramid—as you described your motivation for such varied coursework at the University of Vienna. After anthropology, there was art, restoration, and even psychology. This last course you studied with Hubert Rohracher, who was born in East Tirol but taught in Vienna.[8] From today's point of view, you see these studies also as an attempt to escape your final decision to become a monk. I remember that you once told me how heavy another reason weighed: at the time, you felt yourself to be anticlerical, in the sense of seeing the Church as still having many very bourgeois aspects. That was the sense in which the *Neuland* movement was anticlerical; not antireligious and certainly pious, but anticlerical in its rejection of the old, ivory-tower Catholic system.

DSR: For me, the monasteries were largely part of that outdated system, at least as far as I knew any. The only monastery I felt at home in was Heiligenkreuz Abbey, where Father Walter Schücker was my spiritual counselor.[9] But because my enthusiasm had been awakened by the *Rule of St. Benedict*, I always longed for a monastery that followed the original Rule. That, admittedly, was very cerebral.

JK: What did you hope for from this "back-to-the-roots" approach?

DSR: I do not believe I pictured anything precise. I knew more what I did not want than what I did. And I did not want what I had seen.

JK: Such as? What did you not want?

DSR: An abbey with so many priests that you really become more of a priest than a monk. My idea was if only one could truly go back to the original ways of putting it in practice, without all this historical baggage, then that would be ideal. That was what I told my friend, Father Phillip Walsh, an Oratorian in the United States. In response, he told me of a newly founded monastery that had made precisely that their goal. That was the first time I had heard of Mount Saviour.

JK: We'll get back to that. I want to take a closer look at the time of your early twenties. You spent a relatively long period in East Tirol, on the Kerschbaumer Alm, an Alpine farm, surrounded by the silence of the mountains. On reflection, you could see that time as an incubation period for your later life as a monk. On the Alm, the dividedness may have lifted. Life there is simple and clear; things like daily rhythms, the weather, the animals, the water, milk, cheese, meat, and bread. It is easier to retreat there, there is little distraction. But when you come back down into the valley with its varied ways of living, all the temptations return. And one can't live up on the mountain indefinitely. To a certain degree, that was a symbol of your dividedness or ambivalence back then, which lasted quite a while into your subsequent years.

DSR: The thing about the Alm that was so beautiful to me was the opportunity to explore deeply. And what was so beautiful about the valley was the possibility of breadth. This was the time when I was first able to travel. I was in Switzerland, where everything was a discovery for me—a land of peace and plenty. Together with two friends to whom I still have a close connection—Werner Scholz, the former choirboy, and Heinz Thonhauser from Linz—I went on a bicycle tour. We rode through East Tirol into Switzerland and to the lakes in the north of Italy. We experienced that as a liberating discovery. Today, it is hard to imagine what it meant to us after the war to see the world and be free and mobile enough to simply ride a bike to wherever one wanted to go. Those were significant experiences of breadth. And that was my conflict as well: whether to go deep or broad.

JK: Returning to the Alm was the first place where contemplative life was possible in the form of a "natural monastery." Nature itself was the monastery, that experience of solitude.

DSR: I would call it the experience of a reflective life. On the Alm, I experienced a time of joyous meditation—throughout the entire day. I was either filled with joy at nature or with joy at the little Bible that I carried around with me and could read at any time.

JK: So, you read the book of nature and the books of the Bible?

DSR: I did not think of it in those terms at the time, but St. Bernard of Clairvaux did say that there are these two books in which we can find God. The book of the Holy Scriptures and the book of nature.

JK: And what you perused, so to speak, in East Tirol was the book of nature?

DSR: Yes. There is nothing more beautiful than on the Kerschbaumer Alm, completely cut off from the world; there was not a single person there aside from us all summer. Only once or twice did pilgrims come by; there was a border closing in Italy at the time. All around the Alm meadow, I could see the delicately carved peaks of the Dolomite mountains, white against blue sky...unbelievable.

JK: Here it is again, that encounter with the wonderful as you knew it from your early childhood, when, with your father's help, you look into a tulip and are transfixed by what you find.

DSR: The entire Alm was like a blossom, with the surrounding mountain peaks as petals and us sitting in the middle.

Decision

JK: After your second journey to the United States, you followed your family to America in 1951. Your relatives had already immigrated there and were living in Manhattan, New York. But the question of finally deciding whether to become a monk would not let you go. It is an irony of history that, in the land of possibility, you finally found your possibility, a monastery of your choice in Elmira, where the Benedictine monastery community of Mount Saviour had been founded three years earlier. What drew you to Mount Saviour and finally strengthened you in your decision that becoming a monk really was your path?

DSR: The only important question for me was whether the *Rule of St. Benedict* was truly lived there. That was all. Ideologically, I was completely caught up in this thinking. I was at Mount Saviour for only one afternoon before I joined the community. I arrived around midday, and in the afternoon, I was already sent to plant pumpkins with Father Placid. That gave me the chance to ask him, "Do you really want to return to the *Rule of St. Benedict* here, without modern additions?" His answer was yes. My second question was, "Do you have lay brothers who are separated from the other monks, or are all monks considered equal?" For me those two questions were the touchstone. In the middle ages, they introduced the notion of lay brothers, which resulted in two separate levels in monasteries. To my mind, that ran counter to original Benedictine monastery life, which is why for me it was a touchstone of dedication to the Rule. And again, the answer to my question was satisfactory: "We are all one here and see ourselves as lay brothers. We have only as many priests as the monastery requires." That was enough for me. My motivations were very cerebral, but they set me on the right path. I could make the decisive step, and it is a step I have never regretted. Even errors can bring us to the place where we want to be and should be. In fact, the decision had already been made seven years earlier with the image of the judgment of Solomon.

I Am Because of You

JK: I want to go back for a moment to ask a hypothetical question. In the Solomonic parable, that wholeness, undividedness that showed you a path could also have gone another way. Imagine you had fallen head-over-heels in love with a fascinating woman, and she with you. And imagine that you had not cared about overpopulation and you had said, "We want a family with twelve children." Might that not conceivably have been a way of living in wholeness?

DSR: I suppose that is conceivable. But when I think back, I cannot feel my way into that image. In the first place, that is not how it occurred, and from the first experience in Salzburg onward, I was very inclined in the direction of the monastery. Not in any way that I was constantly thinking of it, not at all. I did truly remain open to other things. But within, I was leaning heavily in that direction.

JK: If I remember correctly, in a former encounter, you said, "After the war, I had two paths; either the right woman comes along or the right monastery. And the right monastery just happened to come along first."

DSR: That was more of a joke that I have made frequently. But in my heart, I did know that if the right monastery comes along, everything will fit. My question was more along these lines: Does such a monastery even exist?

JK: Reflecting critically at your early days, would you consider yourself slightly fundamentalist?

DSR: Much more legalist, and of course that gave me the greatest difficulties in my life as a young monk—because Mount Saviour never seemed to me sufficiently strict or observant of the rules. I would have become a great legalist if fate had not dashed that in the form of disillusionment. But each disillusionment frees us from an illusion. There simply is no monastery that lives as close to the Rule as I wished, and perhaps still wish, deep down. For example, as a young monk I spent days, weeks, and months calculating and writing down what a continuously changing daily schedule might look like, because the angle of the sun changes constantly, and Benedictine monks originally had sundials. That of course would not have fit with the guests who wanted to visit us or come to mass at a specific time. I engaged such questions a great deal. I could still dream of living with stricter observance of the rules than is the case today.

JK: That speaks to the fact that rules, specifically the *Rule of St. Benedict*, gave you stability in those early days as a monk. You seem to have needed something you could hold on to, to structure your own personality, your own life.

DSR: Fixed structures have always been important to me.

JK: Why?

DSR: I think it is a predisposition, even a bodily predisposition.

JK: Because in other things you are also an artistically and poetically talented person, open for art, for the unregulated, so to speak. That is the other side.

DSR: I can see both sides. As early as the war, we were reading Paul Claudel, *The Satin Slipper*.[10] I believe it contains the sentence, "Order is the joy of sense, and chaos is the bliss of imagination." That was an important sentence for me. I had to learn to live with this tension and am still learning to do so. I stood in the middle of this tension.

JK: You could embrace both?

DSR: I was not able to, but I learned and am learning that both are equally important: order and chaos, sense and imagination.

Kerschbaumer Alm

4

BECOMING A MONK

1956–1966

I summed up what becoming a monk means to me in one of those answers that one sometimes gives without even having to think about them. Two or three years have passed since I have entered the monastery, and a friend asks me, "So what do you actually *do* at a monastery all day?" Without hesitation, I hear myself answer, "We stand around the altar and sing thanks and praise. From there, if necessary, we go outside to do our tasks. But we always return to communal prayer as the center of our life."

As indicated by Benedict in his Rule, in those days at Mount Saviour, we prayed the canonical hours seven times a day and once at night. We also prayed the so-called minor hours—Prime, Terce, Sext, and None—separately, not as one prayer, as is the case in some other monasteries. Instead, the bell really did call us together for prayer seven times a day, even for brief prayer periods. Every hour, the changing light colored not only the landscape, but our moods and prayers as well. From around the altar, our communal praise of God radiated into everything else I may do as a monk in between the prayers. Praying to God, however, is already a highly dynamic action in and of itself; a lifelong, continuously deepening process of insight and increasingly grateful praising. Through this process of growth, the entire life of a monk consists in *becoming* a monk.

"Praising, that's it!" writes Rainer Maria Rilke.[1] With this call he is drawing attention to three things: the calling of the poet, the task of the human being itself, and the innermost nature of the Word that arises out of Silence for the sake of praising—and for the sake of nothing else. Growing into this tripartite truth of poetry, humanity, and Mystery as Word (Logos) seems to me to have a central importance in becoming a monk. Yes, a relationship with poetry is part of it. It is no coincidence that Cardinal Newman saw the poetic view of the world as the Benedictine Order's characteristic contribution to Christianity's intellectual history.[2] The monk is by his very humanity a poet, just like Adam giving every animal its name,[3] simply by being a person whose innermost self is the praising Logos. The life of a monk allows us to make praising itself the center, and to let its energy radiate into all areas as joy.

Admittedly, it is then reasonable to ask, "And how do you spend the rest of your time, in which you are not singing the Hours?" The short answer is that the life of a monk is astonishingly varied. Our two main areas of work are study and handiwork—that is to say, working with heart and hand, respectively. Our Prior, Father Damasus Winzen, repeatedly emphasizes that, in our daily studies, we must use our rational minds fully, but at the same time, open our hearts wide. To contemplative reading, or *lectio divina*, are added classes in scholastic philosophy and theology (with rigorous exams). Our brothers, who have themselves only recently finished their studies at the Benedictine college of Sant' Anselmo in Rome, are our professors for those hours. In our library, I can consult the latest books and journals at any time. Father Damasus is in charge there. He also regularly holds courses, since he sees the role of an abbot not as that of an administrator, but as that of a teacher—and I eagerly take notes, to penetrate as deeply as possible into the *doctrina abbatis*. It is true that monastery life is not without its hardships, and for me that includes having to get up early (at that time, just past 4:00 a.m.). I have never been able to get used to that. Father Damasus enjoys telling the story of an extremely well-read young man who—having already written a book about monastic life—became a novice at Father Damasus's former abbey of Maria Laach. He too found the rough reality difficult to adjust to: when the person in charge of waking up the monks—elegantly called the *excitator* in Latin—knocked on his door in the morning with the words "*Benedicamus domino!*" (Let us praise the Lord!), the novice answered not with the prescribed response of "*Deo gratias!*" (Thanks be to God!), but grunted, half asleep, "This is a dog's life!" (He apparently did not last long.)

Since Mount Saviour does not yet have its own novitiate, we novices are sent to Saint-Benoît-du-Lac, a Canadian abbey. The brothers there speak French, which leads to several small confusions. The young monk who is assigned to me as my advisor and French teacher has a stutter. Only years later do I find out that in French, the linden tree is called *tilleul*, and not "*ti-tilleul*." Another time, I must publicly confess that I have shattered a light bulb, but I am unsure of my vocabulary and instead admit to having broken a matchstick. The abbot, Dom Odule Sylvain, sees the ringing laughter that greets this pronouncement as sufficient punishment for my transgression. (In those days, we still did have to publicly confess our sins at the so-called *capitulum culpae*, and as penance we self-flagellated in our cells on Friday evenings while reciting the *Miserere*, Psalm 51.) The abbot is a man whom I learn to esteem and admire. On high Holy Days, he embodies the role of *tres révérend pere*, whom we lead in solemn procession from his rooms to the chapel, where he is robed, piece by piece, in his vestments. On weekdays, however, he stands high up on the ladder as we harvest apples, or lies on the floor of the bathroom mending a pipe—for he is also a plumber.

Becoming a Monk

Saint-Benoît-du-Lac is famous for its Latin singing tradition, and we novices are trained in the spirit of Solesmes, the leading center of the practice.[4] For my entire life, this singing in the service has remained one of the greatest gifts of monastery life. The long, high church does not clearly designate the altar as the central fount of life for the monastic community, but the altar remains so nonetheless.

In French Canada, I learn to live and love the Benedictine tradition in its richest form. We novices are grateful for that, but we are also happy when we can return to our humble monastery back home. Our daily work there is varied. We do not hire help, but do all the chores of the house and garden, the kitchen, the fields, and the stable ourselves. Since Brother Laurence is the only one apart from me who knows how to milk, I am frequently in the stables and enjoy my time there. I am also responsible for our "depot," the pantry from which the brothers can request what they need—notebooks, sandal straps, toothpaste, and so on. We take turns cooking. Cooks and kitchen helpers receive a special blessing when they finish their turns on Sunday. In a stroke of luck for my fellow brethren, I am never made "first cook" but only ever kitchen helper: at home, my brothers and I learned a great many household skills, including even knitting and crocheting, but food was so precious that my mother could not risk potentially spoiling it by letting us attempt to cook.

The construction of new buildings offers many opportunities for my artistic craft. We sleep in the hay loft and escape to the old farm house only in the depths of winter; there it does become quite cramped for us all. So, we must build, but always have a few volunteer helpers. Some of them are professionals, such as Rocko, a skilled carpenter. Alone we would not be able to manage it. The Boy Scouts help as well, and we plant thousands of trees together.

Each morning, during Prime, we receive our work tasks for the day. There are sometimes surprising jobs: one time, I am sent all the way to Connecticut with Brother Ildefons to pick up huge quantities of canned food that are still usable but no longer allowed to be sold after a flood in the warehouse. But my favorite task is being at home cleaning. There is always enough work, and it is less popular with the others. I find it gives me the opportunity for immense, silent wonder. A three-line poem from this time expresses that experience:

> *Broom becomes mallet*
> *The dustpan becomes the gong.*
> *Ah! Little sun dust!*

At the time, the small dustpans were still brass, and the handles of the small brooms were still wood—today, the sound of plastic on plastic would hardly cause mystical enchantment. But in me, that homely gong tone accesses that mysterious realm that Rilke calls "inner world-space," when he writes, "One single space pervades all beings here: / an inner world-space."[5] The outer reaches of space, which we might sense in a bitingly cold winter's night, are expressions of that same reality. This experience is behind a different poem from my time as a young monk, possibly the oldest that I have kept:

> *While the brothers sleep*
> *Orion guards high above*
> *In the winter sky*

Every year, my family visits the monastery for Easter to join in celebrating the festive liturgy. There is complete silence during Holy Week; we greet one another only very briefly. But on Easter Sunday, we celebrate. My grandmother is still with us in the early years—later, her great-grandchildren carry a lantern bearing the Easter fire to the cemetery on the hill above the monastery, and by her grass-covered grave, we hold a festive picnic with Easter eggs.

Becoming a Monk

Our community has many friends. Most of them come from close by, but no small number also visit from further away. They bring us home baked food and many other things that are valuable to us, but they also bring their sorrow and suffering. In most households, pain and desperation come only every once in a while, but in the monastery, all difficult things are offered to us daily, that we may pray for help. I must learn to include these darker sides of life in my praising. Rilke writes, "Only he whose bright lyre / has sounded in shadows / may, looking onward, restore / his infinite praise."[6] "Infinite praise"—that is a good description of our communally sung prayers. Not only because they take part in the song of praise that the Logos sings outside of time, but also because they stop at nothing, exclude nothing, not even the things that grieve us. That is how I want to learn to sing. I believe that we have passed the hardest test of becoming a monk only when we can say, "Between the hammers our heart / endures, just as the tongue does / between the teeth and, despite that, / still is able to praise."[7]

The canonical Hours have not been so obviously the center of communal life in every monastery that I have encountered; but in all of them, the altar was the source of the entire life force of the community. I experience it as a great gift that, unlike some others, I did not have to search from monastery to monastery but instead had such clear "love at first sight" for Mount Saviour. Nevertheless, I was able to encounter many other monasteries. Even as a student, Heiligenkreuz Abbey was my spiritual home because Father Walter Schücker accompanied me as a spiritual counselor there. Under Abbot Karl, Heiligenkreuz was open to experiments at the time and earnestly considered opening a Cistercian cloister in Tibet. In 1951, however, with the Chinese annexation of Tibet, the negotiations ended abruptly.

I did have the opportunity of witnessing an unusual attempt to found a monastery. Around 1980, I got to know three young men who had grown up in the throes of Californian counterculture.

I Am Because of You

They had so seriously thought through the questioning of majority norms and values that they had concluded that only as monks would they be able to authentically realize their positions. And so, they simply set out to found a monastery on their own. They then sought an ecclesiastical connection, and first knocked on the doors of the Anglican Church. There, no one had any idea of what to do with "wannabe monks." The Roman Catholic bishop was also slightly embarrassed, but exhibited a rather benign attitude—after all, the three had lived a relatively strict life following the *Rule of St. Benedict* for years now. They had found an abandoned monastery building and lived there in exchange for custodial duties in the building and grounds. They now asked whether Mount Saviour could help them in any way. At the time, our prior was Father Martin Boler. He went to California for several days, found the young monks trustworthy, and suggested that after a year as novices at Mount Saviour, they could become an independent priory. I was to oversee their novitiate. Unfortunately, I still had several obligations to carry out, and in the meantime, the three had been offered positions in prison pastoral care. They achieved great things there, but it was the end of their plans to found a monastery.

For me, however, the experience led to a fateful turn: These three young men now no longer required me. Instead, their spiritual companion for years, Father Bruno Barnhart, prior of the New Camaldoli Hermitage, said, "We need you with us in Big Sur," and so began my stay in New Camaldoli, which was to last fourteen years. This "hermitage" was set up differently from the other monasteries I knew. Communal living was reduced to a minimum; we monks lived in separate little houses and tended our own gardens. In the one entrusted to me, I planted two fig trees, black bamboo, and nine different kinds of lavender. Before me—and hundreds of meters below—lay the quiet Pacific Ocean. Its blue enormity seemed to rise steeply into the sky. Nowhere have I ever felt more at ease in diving into the inner world-space.

But here too, the monastic community stood around the altar as center and source of strength for daily celebrations of the Eucharist.

Once more, in my old days, I will live in a monastery in which the altar represents the center of life: in the European monastery of Gut Aich. Here, the form of monastic life recalls the image of concentric circles: healing power radiates outward from the altar to the inner ring of the monastery community. Around that ring is crowded the village community of Winkl, as the monastery is in the center of the village. A further ring is formed by the oblates: men and women who are closely connected to the monastery in the Benedictine spirit but often live far away. The furthest circle is made up of those seeking inner and outer health here. A monastery is meant to be for the Church what the Church is meant to be for the world: a place of healing. There are rooms to unburden the sufferings of one's soul, but also herb gardens, the distillation of herbal remedies, a sanatorium consecrated to Hildegard of Bingen, and a center for monastic medicine. As early as the third and fourth centuries AD, Christian monks were referred to as *therapeutes*—healers. Healing means making someone whole, one in themselves, and the word *monachos* (monk) contains the root *monos*, which means not only "alone," but also indicates the oneness of the community and the oneness of all things in the power of the eternal center.

DIALOGUE

JK: Brother David, your birth name is Franz Kuno Steindl. How did you come by the name David?

DSR: David is my name as a monk. We were given new names at the beginning of our novitiate. In truth, I had always wished for the name David, because I had read Kings and Samuel on the Kerschbaumer Alm and all the stories about David. So, for me, David became a heroic figure, which is why I wanted that as a name. But in the Mount Saviour Monastery community, we already had a Brother David, and so I had given up hoping. But shortly before I became a novice, the other Brother David left the community, and it was frequently the case that the new novice received the name of the brother who had just left. It was my good fortune that this also happened with me. At the time, we could not choose our names, and so I had not told anyone that David was my wish. It was a great surprise and joy to me in the end to know that I would be called David.

JK: You discovered some of the silence of the Kerschbaumer Alm at Mount Saviour, which lies in a secluded area once inhabited by the Iroquois. You led a purely contemplative life there, a life that I suspect makes it possible to experience a different, completely new way of being in time. All our lives, *being* and *time* are given to us as an inescapable set of occurrences. But once we discover it, it is like the experience of a wellspring revealing something primeval and incomprehensible. How were you able to experience the phenomenon of time more deeply?

DSR: The guests who visit the monastery often say that time stands still there. One of the aspects of the stillness, or silence, one finds and cultivates in monasteries is also that time stands still in a way. This means avoiding haste and rush, so that ideally one lives in the moment. In fact, that is the decisive factor. But it also includes the subdivision of time by the bell. In monasteries, bells are always very important: they call to prayer. That is something beautiful, uplifting. We were always told to stop what we were doing at the first stroke of the bell. If you are writing, do not dot the i's and cross the t's, even if you have just put the vertical stroke to paper. Stop, stop immediately if it is time! All work in the monastery is done only so long as there is time—and prayer is done in its time as well, not when you feel like it. Conforming to a given ordering of time, and thus also to the cosmic procession of daytimes, enables one to experience one's relationship with time very differently.

JK: On the one hand, time in monasteries is externally organized and structured. But within that structure, it is also possible to experience that different quality of time of which we have already spoken.

DSR: I think that it is precisely through that structured framework that one can transcend time and be in the moment. When we are in the moment, in the Now, we are simultaneously *in* time and *outside* of time.

JK: Why is that?

DSR: We always picture the Now incorrectly, as a short period of time. If that were the case, then it would in theory be possible to halve this short period. That would leave one half that is of the past; that half is not, because it is no longer. The other half would belong to the future, and that half is not, because it is not yet. If we think of a period of time, no matter how short, it is still conceivably possible to subdivide it. But then where is the Now? We see that it cannot truly be found in time at all. Nevertheless, we know what Now means. Understood correctly, the Now is not in time. Rather, time is within the Now. Because when we remember the past, it is now; when the future comes, we will feel it not as the future but also as the Now. So "all is always now," as T. S. Eliot writes.[8]

JK: If my life is existence, then it is spread out into the past, which is in some ways always present. My education, my relationship with my parents, my life experience—everything that has happened in my life is present in some way. I can even repeat and revise it in my memories. But my existence also inevitably reaches into what is coming. That is a significant insight: I can give future to past things. I give some things future, but not to many other things.

DSR: One might say that our experience enriches the Now: my personal Now is enriched by everything I have experienced in the past.

JK: Enriched, yes, but by being open for what is past, I am also in the Now. I open myself to some things and thus give these past experiences a future and new significance.

DSR: ...the possibility of a future.

JK: Conversely, one might also say that the future, meaning what I act in reference to, also intentionally determines my presence, my being, and my becoming. When you decided to become a monk, you were intentionally giving a future to things that had been. That decision then determined all your future becoming.

DSR: Raimon Panikkar has said, "The future does not come later. When it comes, it is now and not later."[9]

JK: If one wants to say something reliable about the Divine, one cannot do so without having had an experience of *being* and *time*. Without temporal experience and experience of creation, all faith is baseless and hollow. Therefore, one needs to understand what creation is, what time is—not necessarily philosophically or intellectually, intuitively works as well. In your personal experience, what is the foundation of a good faith?

DSR: I would phrase my answer like this: faith is radical trust—trust in life and trust in God. We are here speaking of faith in the fullest sense, not merely "believing in something," considering something to be true, which is something completely different from faith. We sometimes imagine that faith stands ready, like a train we just need to board, and then it will bring us to our destination. But it is not that simple. Going forward in faith means, one might say, having the trust to walk on water. The life of faith is a continual test of trust.

JK: One could say our entire life is continually being put to the test?

DSR: Yes, it is put to the test, and articles or sentences of faith can be hints, possible sources of support and help, but sometimes also challenges to this life of trust.

JK: You described your life at the Mount Saviour Monastery community as a strictly regulated daily schedule of prayer, praising God, handiwork, and study. Can you remember any texts that you studied at the time, and whether there were any that had special influence on your development as a monk?

DSR: Yes. We studied strictly according to scholastic philosophy and theology. Our textbook was Joseph Gredt's *Elements of Aristotelian-Thomist Philosophy*.[10] Often, we would memorize entire passages and definitions from it in Latin, for which I am still grateful today. It gave us a clear framework for philosophical thinking. Even once one understands that any frame is limiting and one must continually go beyond it, it is still a great help to have an intellectual framework that clearly confronts fundamental questions and sets one on a path toward answering them. It is good to have such a fundamental structure, and for me that was terribly helpful. The point, after all, is not to study philosophy by reading one philosopher or another; but to find a fundamental orientation for standing in the world. That was very important for me.

JK: And that was possible?

DSR: Yes, the structure we were given was the traditional framework of scholastic and neo-Scholastic thought. But even then, openness was a constant subject: one can go beyond the frame. What we can cloak in terminology is not the final reality. Reality always goes beyond the expressible.

JK: What spiritual texts influenced you at the time?

DSR: We read primarily the Cappadocian Fathers.

JK: Evagrius Ponticus?[11]

DSR: Especially Evagrius, but also the sayings of the fathers, the *Apophthegmata.*[12]

JK: Was that helpful for you at the time? I ask because these texts originated in the completely different time, culture, and reality of late antiquity.

DSR: That was very close to life. We lived in that spirituality. But we also read many Jewish texts, such as writing by Samson Raphael Hirsch, a great German rabbi from the nineteenth century.[13] Father Damasus, our abbot at the time, cited him constantly. Sometimes, he even misspoke and said, "The Holy Samson says…"

JK: You developed a special love of Gregorian chant during your time at the Canadian monastery of Saint-Benoît-du-Lac. This formal, simple way of singing is nearly two thousand years old, and it is thought to go back to the singing in Jewish synagogues. In one of Abraham Joshua Heschel's poems, there is a description of how the world calls for the air to be steeped in delighted songs for God.[14] Gregorian chant comes out of silence and is the Word, sung. What exactly fascinates you about it?

DSR: Gregorian chant has its very particular beauty within the realm of music history as well. It is still sung in the church modes; major and minor did not exist yet. As young monks, we studied this rather difficult way of singing intensively. These chants have an unbelievable beauty, and that beauty is really what draws me to them most. It is a beauty that straddles the border between the sensual and the transcendental. When I think of the most beautiful polyphony of later ages, such as Palestrina, Orlando di Lasso, or Jacobus Gallus, that is what comes closest. After Gregorian chant, polyphony is my favorite music. That is the transfixing thing about the chorale: it is both sensual and transcendental.

JK: Is that due to its simplicity of structure, which leaves space for other things?

DSR: That is certainly part of it. The unison singing, for example, plays a major role, even though I also love the music of the Eastern Orthodox churches, where it is more the harmony taking that role. In Mount Saviour, we also learned and celebrated the Orthodox liturgy. We had a friend who had been ordained in that Eastern tradition, and we often celebrated those long liturgies together with him. That is also incredibly beautiful, very uplifting, bordering on the transcendental. The beauty of singing, especially, is one of the things that often moves people to visit a monastery.

JK: You spoke of the monastery having many friends that support it. Is that equally true of what we might call the "seat of your old age," the Gut Aich monastery in Austria? People come not so much out of curiosity as bringing their life, their sorrows, their suffering. They find support in the monastery, including through intercessory prayer. This is where I would like to pause for a moment, because prayer and active help are often contrasted with one another: Here is prayer, there is real life. This is where we pray, that is where we act. Or along the lines of "All we can do now is pray." What does prayer mean to you personally? Where do you see the help and power of prayer, and how can we pray appropriately without childishly projecting onto God what we ourselves need to be doing and changing?

I Am Because of You

DSR: Prayer in all its forms does not mean primarily coming before God and asking him for something. That is how it is often misunderstood. Instead, it is much more being open to the Great Mystery, to God. This changes us and through us changes the conditions of our life, as well. Any small change we make in this great network of the world and of life influences all others. When we open ourselves to the Divine Mystery in prayer, then we are orienting ourselves in the direction of this Mystery. That is the surprising thing, that life does have a direction. Life wants certain things and does not want others. Life wants aliveness, change, variety, cooperation; all those things are part of the direction of life. And anything that resists those things goes against the grain. Life is an expression of the Great Mystery and the locus of our encounter with the Mystery. By adopting the correct attitude toward life, we are changing the world for the better. In the Lord's Prayer, our first appeal is "Thy will be done," and only then do we pray for our daily bread. That already informs us that we should first orient ourselves along the direction of life, which shows us God's will, and then have the courage to articulate clearly how we imagine the realization we are working toward. But most often, we come to prayer the other way around; one is praying for something and says, "Please, make this happen, and if all things fail, well, then your will be done." That is how it usually is.

JK: You have often said in encounters that—and this was what suggested the question to me—after your parents' divorce, you had prayed a great deal for your parents to be reunited. Now, I can imagine children who pray as you did, who are, in their experience, not heard by God, and then despair completely over God and want nothing more to do with God. In their eyes, one might say God has become powerless. They feel that they have not done anything wrong. How was that for you? Why didn't you lose your faith when your prayers could not achieve what you wished for so strongly in secret?

DSR: I think it was a great gift in that I was introduced to trust in God from the very beginning. We had talked about that already. This trust became so fundamental to me that it was not shaken even when God appeared not to hear my prayer. Perhaps I could also have said what I later heard from a different child: "God did hear my prayer, but unfortunately he said no." If upbringing has not rooted one to trust in God, then one is likely to say, "If there is a kind God at all, then he is obligated to fulfill my request." This was not the case for me. In the same way, children, who ask their parents for something that the parents then deny them, maybe even a hundred times, do not lose their faith in their parents. It was quite similar with me.

JK: To return to the fundamental question: What does the power of prayer consist of, to you, if we are not convincing, persuading, and in some way manipulating God? What is it that makes it good, indeed a central Christian virtue, to pray every day and to live in prayer?

DSR: I can speak only based on my experience, which I might not have caught up with yet. Energy—life energy—flows through this web of life in which we stand, and we channel this energy in a particular direction using our prayers. That is all part of our freedom, but it can be proved only in personal experience. For me, that is not a question; I have been fortunate to experience it personally. I also feel when people pray for me, and am deeply grateful for it. I know how much of what I succeed in doing, how much of my health and all other things, I owe only to that God-given life energy that is bestowed on me through so many loving hearts. This conviction is a little beyond rational, I admit it. It extends past what is rationally provable. But we are also considering a topic that goes beyond reason.

JK: Nevertheless, in prayer one runs the risk of becoming childish, imagining it very childishly. I don't mean as a child, but as an adult, not seeing how one must change, what one can do to alter one's own life. There is also the danger of spiritualizing problems that are solvable only on other levels. But as a spiritual adviser, you know firsthand that one needs to distinguish very clearly between those. My point is that one should avoid escaping into prayer when what one really needs to do is confront important changes in one's own life. That would be a kind of "misuse" of prayer.

DSR: Yes, that is a widespread fault. Prayer depends on facing the Mystery, facing life again and again. If we do that, life will tell us what we need to add. Rilke formulates a poetic call for facing life in this way in his famous poem "Archaic Torso of Apollo." In it, the ancient sculpture confronts us with such immediacy that we are "all eyes," as it were. Then, suddenly, one and a half lines before the end of the poem, he turns and calls to us: "For here there is no place / that does not see you." And then the challenge: "You must change your life."[15] If we really face up to life—be it in art, in nature, or in spirituality—then we inevitably come to the point where we must change our life. That point is also the watershed in praying.

JK: Human cohabitation always means being confronted with problems and, one hopes, growing through them. Franz Kafka once illustrated it using the example of love: "Love is as unproblematic as a vehicle. All that is problematic are the drivers, the passengers, and the road." So once a problem has been solved, a new one appears immediately. Some people think of faith as a kind of transcendental insurance policy against inherent problems—religion as solving all problems. How do you see it?

DSR: Faith is trust in life, lived new again and again—new in each moment because life is also changing every moment. Faith is the opposite of insurance. It constantly makes us unsure, and without it, we would need no trust. In trust, I know myself assured despite feeling unsure. Nevertheless, the more one feels unsure, the more trust one needs to feel assured.

JK: The Christian religion does not understand itself as a spiritual system of order and insurance, the way some people imagine it—that one can flee from life's uncertainties into religion.

DSR: Religion gives us security by showing us a path to keep trusting in life. There is also so much more to religion than doctrine. That is just a tiny part of it.

JK: More than ethics, as well.

DSR: Community is a part of it. The community supports you and helps to realize this trust in life. That is always the decisive element: trust in life.

JK: In the nineteenth century, Friedrich Nietzsche had a different image of religion. He was heavily polemic against a Christianity that was nihilistically conceived in the sense of a faith that mistakes itself for being convinced, for holding certain positions, for a dogmatic belief. Nietzsche sees this Christianity as a worldview, as a religious ideology. To him, Christianity has become a worldview: "Christianity is Platonism for the 'people.'"[16] Even before university, he encounters Anselm of Canterbury's proof of God, according to which God is the most perfect conceivable being. Anselm concludes that anyone who thinks that God does not exist is not thinking of the most perfect conceivable being, since an existing being is more perfect than a nonexistent being. Therefore, God must exist. While this sounds logical, Nietzsche saw through the apparent logic, identifying it as a mere word game and empty idea of God. He responded to this idea by saying, "God is dead!...We have killed him."[17] This thought-up, imagined stopgap deity is misused for political and moral power—that God no longer exists after Nietzsche. Nietzsche chose the atheist path, presumably because the Christian God he knew from his time seemed ungodly to him. I can imagine that in your years of becoming a monk, you, Brother David, thought a great deal about this atheism—which you were familiar with—and about authentic faith in God—a faith based in experience. What do you see as the foundations of such a faith that does not turn in the direction of atheism but is truly based on experience and is not merely a fantasy that I can choose to have or not?

DSR: Both are necessary. On the one hand, having experience as the ultimate bedrock of faith, and on the other, remembering that anything one can say about this Great Mystery, even if it is completely right, is still more wrong than right. That is the thesis of negative theology, which goes deeper than its positive counterpart.[18] In the end, the Mystery is the Unknowable. And if something is unknowable, then it can also not be put into words. We may experience it by letting it take hold of us, but we cannot ourselves take hold of it. When I was studying theology, however, I was thrilled with the profound creativity of statements on the Trinity. I always saw these speculations as a huge cathedral of thought. But just as God does not live in buildings, the Trinity does not live in thought-palaces. Yet it is something beautiful and does also point in the right direction. But reality simply goes infinitely beyond it. Astonishingly, as humans we do have access to this reality, but in it we also gain insight into the limits and insufficiency of conceptual thought. Something in our thinking touches that which extends beyond thinking, and we experience that not so much as touching but as our being touched. Bernard of Clairvaux said, "Knowledge comes from grasping something, wisdom from being gripped by something." The deepest prayer is being gripped, touched in such a way.

JK: But if I want to share my experience of being gripped, or talk about this being touched in a debate in the social sciences—that is, look at it methodically—I need to think about it. It makes a difference whether I invent something, imagine something, or am speaking from experience. I want to take up the example of the Trinity that you mentioned earlier. One can think of it as a thought game, but I suspect that this is not the actual purpose of a three-part God. It may be "only" an image, but it certainly claims at first to be based on experience, and thus be graspable, explicable, and not the brainchild of a clever theologian trying to unnecessarily complicate Christianity in comparison with Islam. Why would you want to hold on to the image of a tripartite God, and what does it have to do with our experience?

DSR: That is not limited to Christianity. One can find a trinitarian understanding of the Mystery even in primeval human spirituality. There we see the encounter with the Mystery as the "Nothing" from which everything comes. The origin of everything is a leap from Nothing to Being. That Mystery extends beyond Being. In Christianity, we call this deep foundation "Father," because Jesus used that form of address. This "Nothing" gives rise to the fullness of everything. Borrowing from Greek philosophy, we call this the Logos—the Word from out of Silence. The "Nothing" is the Silence from which the Word springs. Everything that is can ultimately be understood as Word, because it speaks to me, and I can answer this address: I can Understand the Word in dutiful action. We Christians call this aspect the Holy Spirit, the Spirit of Understanding through which the Father speaks the Word, which, in turn, becomes the Silence of the Father by dutiful Understanding. In encounters with the Great Mystery, it is always about these three aspects: Silence, Word, and Understanding through action. Those are primeval experiences of human encounters with the Mystery, but these experiences also extend far beyond what can be put into words. We live surrounded by the Mystery. That is beautifully expressed in Paul's statement that "in him we live and move and have our being" (Acts 17:28). *In* God—that needs to be emphasized more in the Christian catechesis.

I Am Because of You

JK: The idea of the *monachos*, the monk, that you touched on above as meaning "being one" or "being at one," also indicates this "being in God." How do we achieve this experience of being at one with everything, and to what degree are we all called to find this inner monk pointing to oneness, even if we are not monks ourselves?

DSR: This call is not external, it is merely how we experience our longing to move from multiplicity into oneness, from noise into Silence, from haste into serenity, from distraction into concentration. This bundle of desires, I would say, is our inner call to monkhood.

JK: How can we realize this "monkhood" in our daily lives? I am thinking particularly of people who have a job and a family—what might the life of a monk look like for them? How can I cultivate this unity that points to oneness with all things?

DSR: Here again it comes down to that one thing: we must learn to be alive in the moment.

JK: What specifically does that mean? Some people understand it as being thoughtless, living day to day, not having a plan...it is easy to misunderstand.

DSR: It means being entirely present in the given moment. Some people, for example, experience it in sports, as that moment during a run when they *are* the run: "being in the flow"—meaning being alive to the moment. It can also happen while baking bread, working at the computer, sawing and hammering at a construction site, doing the dishes, or caring for a sick person. In that sense, a layperson who is consciously aiming to be continuously alive in the Now is a monk, if you will. And a monk who neglects that aspect is hardly worthy of the term *monk*. Monkhood is not primarily a vocation but a form of life, and the significant thing about it is being alive in the Now. Monks are not recognized by their habit but by their efforts to live in the Now. That is true of those wearing the habit, but also of those not wearing it.

JK: That represents a unique way of being a human being. Living in the moment is something not many people do. Martin Heidegger described it very well: nature of everyday existence is falling for things—that is to say, I fall for the next thing, am imagining a future, or stuck in the past. Or I am caught up in what others think of me or what they wear, what they are doing. Falling for the "oughts" ("I ought to do this, you ought not to do that"). The contrary model is to be present, to actively be, to be alive in the moment.

DSR: Monks, though, can fall for things in this way too. And there is something else that is important: monks live in communities. Even the hermit belongs to a community, though in a less obvious form. That is why I hope for good monasteries, good monastic communities that manage to put into practice what we urgently need in this world. On a journey by coach, someone pointed out a monastery to Francis de Sales, saying, "In this monastery live saintly monks." His response was, "I would prefer it if you could say, 'That is a saintly monastery.'"

With my grandmother

5

INTERFAITH DIALOGUE

1966–1976

How on earth have I wound up in this far-flung place in the wilds of California? In every direction, I would have to walk several days in these gorges to find another human dwelling. Tassajara lies at the deepest point of a valley, so deep that, in the winter, the sun shines down on it for barely an hour. Over two mountains and a perilously narrow gravel road, we come to these few carefully tended huts reminiscent of a small Japanese village. There are also three somewhat larger buildings. These are the remnants of a spa hotel built a hundred years ago from the rocks of the stream by Chinese immigrant laborers, who also built the road. For thousands of years, Native Americans have sought healing in the hot springs that bubble up here.

But why have I come to this first Zen monastery outside of Japan, given that I never even wanted to leave Mount Saviour? I smile when I remember how much I enjoyed picturing myself in twenty years—say, on a Friday in 1980—standing on the very same spot, and praying the exact same Friday psalm for Terce as in the previous years. The idea that the future might be so reliably predictable gave me a wonderful feeling of being protected.

My mother told me that, as a baby, I was happiest when swaddled tightly and bound closely. Even then, one could see what stability meant to me. What others find monotonous, such as stuffing envelopes with monastery circulars for hours, I find highly satisfying. I feel safe in repetition; it feels like the mirroring of eternity in the midst of time and gives me something to hold on to. I was happy and satisfied at Mount Saviour and did not, under any circumstances, want to leave or want change. Maybe for that very reason, life had to teach me that the *stabilitas*, which I swore in my monastic vows, did not mean sedentary living, but unbroken belonging to the community of brothers. It is said that between the lines of our vows, the hand of God writes what we cannot imagine. Although life does not always give us what we want, it always gives us what we need.

Father Damasus, for example, wanted me to accept the offer of a one-year postdoctoral scholarship at nearby Cornell University because it would lead to friendships with professors who could advise us in agriculture and building the monastery. Professor Norman Daly, especially, was to become a lifelong friend and patron. After twelve years in the monastery, Father Damasus would sometimes send me out to give a lecture, since he could not himself honor every one of the many invitations he received. On one of those occasions, I met the young Zen monk Eido Shimano Roshi—at the time, he was called Tai San—and he invited me to New York City to experience a Zen training in his newly opened Zendo. How I eventually attended is a long story, which I will describe briefly here.

Father Damasus had studied comparative religion under Gustav Mensching, whom he held in great esteem.[1] When a monk of Mount Saviour was invited to study Zen practice, he was thus open to the idea. I liked the plan as well, just not for myself. Even as a student, I had answered colleagues trying to interest me in Buddhism by saying, "Life does not seem to me long enough to enter my own Christian religion deeply enough, do I need to add anything more?" But it was the time of protests over the war in Vietnam, and I had been invited to a rally at the University of Michigan by students there who knew me. I then thought of inviting Tai San. And he had the courage to attend, even though some friends told him that he, as a Japanese person, might be deported. As a Buddhist-Christian team, we made an impression on the media. In the long view, however, the more important result was that, through this occasion, we got to know each other more closely. We had to live together in a small dorm room, but felt more like two goldfish who had already spent years swimming in the same aquarium—completely in rhythm with one another. Thich Nhat Hanh later told me, "We felt closer to the Christians who were monks like we were than we did to Buddhists who were not monks."[2]

After my return to Michigan, I suggested to Father Damasus that we invite Tai San to the monastery. He came for several days, and in the resulting conversations, the brothers asked him theological questions, to which he gave typical Zen answers. They kept talking at cross purposes, and when he left, I thought the entire thing might have been a washout. But to my surprise, the brothers all agreed: "We did not understand his answers, but the way he walks and stands, his overall behavior—he is a true monk!" Shortly thereafter, Father Damasus did indeed send one of us to Tai San, and it turned out to be me after all. So, after two years of living in New York, I was invited, along with other students of the Zen Study Society of New York, to visit this mountain monastery of Tassajara, recently founded by Shunryu Suzuki Roshi.

Again and again, these summer weeks raise the question of why I feel so at home here as a monk. The daily schedule is quite similar to that of Mount Saviour, but instead of praying the canonical Hours, we sit on our pillows in the meditation room and immerse ourselves in what we Christians call the "Prayer of Silence": we let ourselves fall into the deep Silence of the Great Mystery. Silence unites; very soon, we have become a true community. In the same way that the Hours formed the center of our community at Mount Saviour, here it is silent meditation. There, in Christian terms, the Holy Spirit praises the Father in the eternal Word; here, in contrast, the Word returns to Silence, that is, Christ returns to the Father.

In both places, inner movement leads us into one and the same inexplicable Mystery. Later, connecting the different terms of the two will cost me years of intellectual work, but even now I am experiencing this commonality and it fascinates me. In Tassajara, I become conscious of what Thich Nhat Hanh experienced in Vietnam: that our life as monks connects us deeply—above and beyond all our external differences. This commonality is a stable foundation, more convincing than all apparent contradictions.

Today, it is my turn to light a stick of incense in front of the statue of the Buddha. Does that not actually go against my beliefs? Should I be allowed to do so at all? Did early Christians not refuse even to the death to offer frankincense before the likeness of the Roman emperor? Already I am in line and hold the incense in my hand and am still unsure. I think of my ancestors in faith, and my thoughts run into one another. But then they become collected in a single point: the Roman emperor. What stands before me on this altar is not the likeness of the Roman emperor, but a spiritual master who (very much like Jesus) advocated values diametrically opposed to those of the emperor. Buddha as well as Jesus countered the love of power with the power of love. Both built egalitarian communities to protest existing power hierarchies. If I let frankincense rise before the figure of Jesus, why not before a statue of the Buddha? "Yes," says a voice inside me, "but are we not praying to God through Jesus Christ?" Certainly. But just as the cross or the statue point beyond themselves to Jesus Christ and to the Buddha, so Jesus Christ and the Buddha point beyond themselves to the Great Mystery that we Christians call God. It is to this Mystery that the incense of prayer is dedicated in the end. Jesus says, "Why do you call me good? No one is good but God alone" (Luke 18:19). And the Buddha does not even use the word *God* because he wants to keep the Great Mystery unnamed. I focus on this Great Mystery and dedicate my stick of incense to it. I can now do so wholeheartedly.

Back in New York, Tai San and I, together with our friends Swami Satchidananda and Rabbi Joseph Gelberman, found the Center for Spiritual Studies. Our Swami is a guru to hundreds, perhaps thousands of young people. (He also addresses the crowd of 400,000 hippies at 1969's historic Woodstock Festival.) Often, all four of us participate in his religious events. We develop a tested format for our dialogues: following an invitation from a university—at one point we are even invited to Harvard—we hold discussions amongst ourselves on the first day, while on the second, we are available for public lectures and panel discussions.

An unforeseen opportunity for our events soon opens, and one that will prove particularly fruitful: the "House of Prayer" movement, a call for renewal from within the United States Catholic Church. It is driven particularly by women's religious orders, and over the past century, the so-called active orders among them have worked themselves to the vanguard of their respective areas of work. Their schools, hospitals, social organizations are of the highest standard. Now, after the Second Vatican Council, however, these orders begin to look inward, concluding the following: we are professionally trained at the highest level, but the profession of our order requires that we receive a different kind of training—a training of our interior lives.

In 1967, Sister Margaret Brennan, IHM, issues an invitation to discuss this project, and her short advertisement in a religious magazine draws representatives of about a hundred orders to the very first meeting in Monroe, Michigan. Over the next years, the United States sees the creation of countless "Houses of Prayer," places where for days, weeks, or even years, sisters can live, pray, and "recharge their spiritual batteries" together. Frequently, laypeople join as well. They read the works of Christian mystics, and Paulist Press begins to publish its series "Classics of Western

Spirituality," which will go on to span over 150 volumes. But what is still missing are living teachers. For lack of better applicants, we—the Swami, the Rabbi, the Zen monk, and I—attempt to fill this large gap, since the interest in non-Christian spirituality is also significant.

In the last year of his life, Thomas Merton became another adviser of the House of Prayer movement. Through his encounters with Zen Buddhism, he had become a key figure of interfaith dialogue himself. I once asked him whether Buddhism had influenced his understanding of Christian teaching in any decisive ways. Unusually for him, he did not answer my question immediately. After earnest contemplation, he told me that he did now see our Christian faith with new and different eyes. Since Merton's books have influenced the understanding of faith held by hundreds of thousands of readers, that alone is a measure of how this faith movement has touched even Christians who were completely unaware of the fact. I myself was later to write a book in which I presented the Creed in ways that, as bishops assured me, met the strictest standards for orthodoxy—but also allowed the Dalai Lama to identify with its words and even write a preface.[3]

I was privileged to get to know the Dalai Lama at the San Francisco Zen Center on his very first visit to the United States. Even in this first encounter, he showed me how his deep spirituality found unity in things that on the surface seem different. In a small discussion group, someone referred to the emphasis the Christian sermon generally places on suffering and pain, and did so in almost lewd terms: "Your Holiness, Buddhist teaching frees us from suffering. So, what do you have to say to Christians, who have been practically wallowing in the idea of pain for two thousand years?" The Dalai Lama gestured as if to say, not so fast, please! Then, with great seriousness, he answered, "According to Buddhist teaching, suffering is not surmounted by leaving our pain behind us, but by taking on pain to help others." In these words, he was outlining the archetype of Bodhisattva, who attains enlightenment but turns back at the threshold of eternal blessedness and vows not to enter until even the last suffering being has been redeemed. The parallels with Christian teaching of redemption were discussed at the congress "The Christ and the Bodhisattva," which Professor Steven Rockefeller organized in 1986 at Middlebury College in Vermont. I can remember a touching gesture made by the Dalai Lama on that occasion. We were sitting next to one another, listening to a lecture by another guest. He takes my hand, pulls my prayer ring off my finger, and instead, hands me his 108 prayer beads. Without a word of explanation needing to be said, he lets the Christian beads slide through his fingers, and I do the same with the Buddhist ones, until the end of the lecture. In such moments, healing and salvation become reality, no matter which savior we pray to—it can easily be the Messiah as well.

The image of the Messiah shines out in another similar hour of grace, when in 1972, adherents of many religions meet at Mount Saviour. This first great congress of its kind is known as "Word out of Silence," and it attracts Raimon Panikkar, Alan Watts, Archimandrite Kallistos Ware, Pir Vilayat Inayat Khan, as well as practically countless Swamis, Roshis, and Rabbis. To this are added a group of juvenile offenders from the Elmira Correctional Facility who are serving parts of their parole with us in the monastery and dance enthusiastically with all the famous personalities on the lawn. I can no longer remember whether it is the Reb Shlomo Carlebach or the Reb Zalman Schachter who, during our last dinner together, tells a hasidic story that moves us all because it has become truth in our midst: "The learned Rabbi and his students were together, and so strong was the love among them that the Master sent one of them to the window with the words: 'Quickly, look out to the window to see whether the Messiah has come!' 'All outside is as it ever was,' came the disappointed answer. 'But Rabbi,' asked another student, 'would we need to look out the window if the Messiah had come? Would we not know it at once in here also?' 'Yes!' answered the Rabbi, 'but in here the Messiah has already come!'"

What had begun in the 1970s was to culminate at the Parliament of World Religions held in Chicago in 1993. There, Hans Küng provided an impulse for the "Global Ethics Project," which posits that all ethical systems are grounded in something one might call a primeval human ethics.[4] This corresponds to the insight from the field of comparative religion that all religious traditions can be traced back to a certain primeval religiousness shared by all human beings. As people, our innermost selves are oriented toward the Great Mystery to which the word *God* merely wants to point.[5] We experience this Mystery in three ways: as Silence, as Word, and as Understanding. Word, in this sense, is all there is, since we experience it as directed at us: it "speaks to us." Word has its origins in Silence and aims at Understanding. Understanding, in turn, is that dynamic process in which we listen so deeply into the Word that it takes hold of us and leads us back to its source—to Silence. The Cappadocian Fathers of the fourth century referred to this as "the circle dance" of the Trinity.

I put that image at the center of my contribution in Chicago. It can be demonstrated that Silence is just as central to Buddhism as the Word is to Western traditions and as Understanding is to Hinduism. The goal of yoga—the root word of which is related to our word *yoke*—is the connection (or "yoking together") of Word and Silence through Understanding. None of these traditions can grasp the Divine Mystery in its fullness. Together, they form a circle dance, in which—from a Christian perspective—the Logos, the eternal Word, has its origins in the Silence of the Father and returns to the Father in the Understanding of the Holy Spirit. These images, in the end, are completely inadequate, but they ripened what for me had begun as a seed a quarter of a century earlier in Tassajara.

DIALOGUE

JK: Brother David, you have already mentioned that order, rules, repetition give you security within the monastery. And at Mount Saviour in the beginning, you wanted as little change as possible. But then life taught you something else—seen from the outside, there are probably few monks who will later be on the road as much as you. With that, you redefined the monastic idea of *stabilitas loci*.[6] What gives you support and stability in your many travels?

DSR: *Stabilitas loci* is not a Benedictine formula. It is really a misunderstanding, since the actual term is *stabilitas in comunitate*, meaning "a lasting membership in the community," and *that* is what one vows. Since the community generally lives in one place, however, it is naturally the case that one lives there. But due to circumstances, I have lived a different form of life while remaining true to the community—and what is more important, the community has remained true to me. Even though many of my fellow brethren may not have fully understood what it was all about, they still trusted me. This trust is a great gift that I appreciate very much. Continually, I felt inner support, knowing that this community and their prayers carried me and trusted in me. That is, of course, also a major responsibility for doing this trust justice and living the connection with this community that is contained in the vow of *stabilitas in comunitate*.

JK: The stage of your life you have described here is marked by your being sent on lectures and seminars by your abbot. For example, you accepted the invitation of a young Zen monk, Eido Shimano Roshi. After initial skepticism, you eventually learned Zen meditation in his Zendo, and the two of you protested the Vietnam War together as a Christian-Buddhist team. What was the most surprising experience you had when you were first engaging with Zen Buddhism? In the beginning, after all, your position was rather conservatively Christian.

DSR: One important aspect of my encounter with Zen Buddhism was the full realization that the Logos is the focal point of theology in the Christian tradition. It is, after all, *theo*-logy: a speaking about God. A theology that has the Father at its center would have to be a Silence about God. All talking would be beside the point, which cannot be articulated or expressed in human language—which is what Buddhism immerses itself in.

JK: How can one describe the indescribable of this Divine dimension, which in Christianity is called Father?

DSR: There is not much that one can describe. Our Prayer of Silence, which has a long tradition in the history of Christianity, is no different really from Zen meditation. In our silent prayer, we immerse ourselves in the Silence of God, the Great Mystery. And in Buddhism, that is as central as life in God's Word is for us.

JK: Would it be accurate to say that one is diving into the "Dimension of Nothing," into that Nothing from which everything came in the very beginning?

DSR: Yes, that is well put. One approaches this Mystery by opening the ears of the heart for this Great Silence.

JK: But this Divine dimension that we call "Father" in Christianity is also identical with the Nothing. We have access to this Nothing with our senses by simply not seeing what is there, like the source of a wellspring, the existence of which we can only deduce from the water flowing out.

DSR: That is all a question of terminology. In this context, the Nothing is not an empty nothing but it is the hidden fullness of all possibilities. It is a highly pregnant Nothing, pregnant with everything there is. The birth is then the origin of all that exists. But the "it" implied in "all that exists" is not in itself an existing "it."

JK: We cannot recognize, analyze, describe, grasp it. That is what makes us, with our Western mindset, so anxious and uncertain, because we are quick to equate it with nonbeing and death. We fear our destruction in the Nothing, and that feeds our hidden fear of death.

DSR: But that is true of both Zen Buddhist meditation and of silent prayer, because the two cannot really be distinguished.

JK: If I have understood you correctly, what fascinated you about the Buddhist tradition was a spiritual practice that exists in Christianity as well, even if it is currently not as alive, or at least the treasure it represents is not so widely known anymore.

DSR: What fascinated me was that this practice was so central to Zen Buddhism. Buddhists do not speak of God, so in my encounters with Eido Shimano Roshi—then Tai San—I likewise would always avoid speaking of God. I spoke of the prime cause, the ultimate cause of existence. But after a relatively short time, he understood what I was doing and simply started talking about God himself. So, he was speaking of God, and I still avoided using that term. For me, that was proof that we understood one another. He also understood the difference between silence and speech very well. When I would try to express a facet of Buddhist teaching as clearly as possible and then ask, "Have I understood that correctly?" he would only laugh and say, "Very precise, but how sad that you had to put it in words." And conversely, when he would get carried away and begin to talk and explain Buddhism, he would suddenly break off mid-sentence and say, "I am talking too much. I'm almost becoming a real Christian!" Yes, he recognized this contrast very clearly.

Around the same time, I met Swami Satchidananda, and he unlocked a completely different dimension of the Mystery for me, one that is explored and experienced in Hinduism: Understanding. Because Understanding is related essentially to Word and Silence, I suspected early on that it might play the same role in Hinduism as the Word in Christianity and Silence in Buddhism. But this division seemed almost too neat and orderly to be true, until with my own ears, I heard the great Hindu teacher Swami Venkatesananda remark tersely, "Yoga *is* Understanding." In that moment, I was overwhelmed. My suspicion had been confirmed in an instant: Yoga—Hindu spirituality in all its forms—is like a yoke connecting Word with Silence. *Yoke* and *Yoga* share a close linguistic connection. If we listen so deeply into the Word that it takes hold of us and leads us back into the Silence from which it came, then in a dynamic process, Word and Silence become joined as Understanding. In Christian terminology, the Holy Spirit is the Spirit of Understanding. Father, Son, and Holy Ghost; Silence, Word, and Understanding; Buddhist, Christian, and Hindu spirituality—it all fits together incredibly well. And it was given to me not only to experience that intellectually but feel it tangibly in encounters with representatives from these various traditions. That was a great gift.

JK: Then what role does the Christian faith play today in the network of world religions, in today's world? Do you see the Christian faith as one offer among many, or does it have some unique character or claim to truth?

DSR: As a Christian, the Christian faith has a unique claim. As an anthropologist, I see it as the expression of primeval human faith in one of many religious traditions. The ultimate purpose is to practice grappling with the Great Mystery, which occurs within the religions. Christianity, Buddhism, Hinduism are forms of grappling with the Mystery in this way, and for me that happens in the Christian forms that are irreplaceable to me. To a Buddhist, the Buddhist forms are of irreplaceable value.

I Am Because of You

JK: Let's return to Buddhism. There is a central attitude here that one could describe as "beginner's mind"—though that term can easily be misconstrued as talking about the difference between inexperienced pupils and experienced teachers. What is this beginner's mind that became so important to you?

DSR: For example, those who come to each day with a beginner's mind experience it as if it were the first day. To a beginner's mind, each time one brushes one's teeth, one is brushing as if one had never brushed them before. Once one tries it in practice, one starts to see what a difference to life it makes—how interesting, how alive everything suddenly becomes. One sees things that one never noticed before. That is why Buddhist teachers speak of typical everyday living as a kind of sleepwalking. A sleepwalker simply goes through the motions of each twenty-four-hour day, but a waking person experiences life in all its aliveness. Being awake in this sense means living with a beginner's mind. Am I not always a beginner? After all, I have never experienced this new day before.

JK: Nor this encounter—we've spoken with one another several times, and it is always new. We always start something new, explore the still unheard. At any rate, I certainly do feel like a beginner again and again.

DSR: That is good, both of us must do that...

JK: ...with a fresh mind. One could also say that the aim is to continuously understand things newly and more deeply from their origins. To plumb the depths of things, seek out their source and not uncritically adopt the fixed terms, prejudices, intellectual one-way streets, the opinions about people and things, but rather to set them aside and bracket them.

DSR: Putting words to anything is a generalization, sticking it in one drawer or another. If I do not give a name to something, it

100

remains pure experience. That is part of the beginner's mind as well: I do not have the proper name for this yet. But once I name it, I am no longer truly experiencing it. Instead, the name comes between what I am doing and my living experience. It becomes habit. The rabbis say that getting used to something is the true exile. In fact, what was exile? Was it being in Babylon or Egypt? No. They respond that the true exile lies in getting used to things. As soon as we become used to something, we are no longer experiencing it with a beginner's mind but are in exile.

JK: I would like to make a connection with an earlier thought: you have said that you need order, stability, and repetition. How do order, stability, and repetition fit with this beginner's mind, which is always seeking to see, experience, comprehend things anew, living out of that initial experience, as it were?

DSR: Perhaps that is the very reason why repetition—so-called monotonous work—is so dear to me. Several brothers find it boring when we send out our circulars together. But each envelope into which you slip something is new: I have never had this specific circular in my hands before. When we live in the moment, for us that moment becomes surprising and fresh as dew. This insight is possibly also what stands behind God's great promise in the apocalypse: "See, I am making all things new" (Rev 21:5). If we live and move and have our being in God, consciously, then everything is renewed in every moment. It does not mean that "at a certain moment in history, I will renew everything and from that point it will grow old again." Far from it! Instead, it means, "Look here! Wake up! I am making everything new in each moment." That is the great promise. So, there is actually no repetition.

JK: It is paradoxical: we live from a wellspring that is constantly renewed, and yet the origin of this wellspring is beyond our reach; is neither visible nor tangible. That is a good description of the situation in which we live. We cannot hold on to the infinite

Mystery of God, but from out of the beginner's mind, we can discover that there is something that gifts itself to us continuously.

DSR: The origins that lie behind the wellspring are neither wellspring nor source. The beginner's mind regards the wellspring every moment to sense the source.

JK: You extended your knowledge of Zen Buddhism in the mountain retreat of Tassajara, founded in California by Shunryu Suzuki Roshi. You describe a moment there where you were assailed by doubt as to whether you could light incense to honor the image of the Buddha—whether such an action might not actually be a betrayal of your Christian faith. But then you conclude that it is in fact possible. I would like to use that as a jumping-off point to ask, How do you see the person and role of Jesus Christ in comparison with the Buddha?

DSR: In the man Jesus, Christians encounter God in a unique way. The Christian tradition points to Jesus in Pilate's words: *Ecce homo!*—"Behold the man!" In Jesus, we see what it means to be human, and in his image, Christians aim to become fully human. For us Christians, Jesus is the point of access to the Great Mystery. He is the point where the Christian tradition crystallizes— just as the Buddha is in Buddhism.

JK: Although the two play a different role in the concept of the religion. And in their veneration.

DSR: On the surface, more different even than it would appear, but deep down, hardly distinguishable.

JK: Buddhism and Christianity have different notions of salvation. I would be interested to hear how you describe those. To pick up on a scene you related: on a panel with the Dalai Lama, one of the questioners noted a distinction between Buddhism, which aims to transcend suffering, and Christianity, which is supposedly enamored of it. This misunderstanding has a long history and probably goes back to a misinterpretation of Christ's sacrifice, in the sense that he bore the sins of man to reconcile humanity with an angry Father God. How do you see Jesus' sacrifice on the cross, and how should it be viewed in comparison with the Buddhist ideal of Bodhisattva?

DSR: On the surface, the two are quite different. But this surface is only the interpretation of a historical event. What occurs in the Bodhisattva and what occurs in Jesus Christ is, in both cases, a completely radical yes to mutual belonging: to all humans, animals, plants, a yes to mutual belonging even with the Great Mystery. This unbounded yes to mutual belonging is love. Interpretations of that can be very different even within the Christian tradition. In the days when Paul interpreted the death of Jesus as a sacrifice for our sins, that was only one of many interpretations of equal value. But over time its growth has so outpaced the others' that today it predominates in the consciousness of Christians and non-Christians alike. Perhaps it has become so established because the framework of sin and expiation is so deeply rooted in the human ego. Later, Anselm of Canterbury cast this interpretation into a form that seemed to make sense to the feudal society of the time, but today stands in the way of many people's deeper understanding: sin as an insult to God's majesty, which can be expiated only by the death of a man equal to God.

JK: That stems from the Germanic theological tradition of justification.

DSR: Yes. The culture from which it stems has changed, but the formula was passed on unchanged until it not only no longer communicates anything that people can understand but now stands in the way of their understanding. That was unfortunately the case with this doctrine of justification.

JK: But during Lent, for example, we still sing "*All Sünd' hast du getragen, / sonst müssten wir verzagen.*"[7]

DSR: That is precisely what I mean by the passing on of formulas that no longer fit. It is not that the line is wrong; it comes from an interpretation that no longer helps us today, but with which we have many associations that bear fruit. We must really open ourselves up to the sentence "See, I am making all things new." That includes our interpretation of Jesus' death and resurrection.

JK: But the question behind it—I would like to take up this motif, at least—is the question of whether there needs to be a sacrifice. We know that life also means sacrificing. And I do not mean in the sense of a scapegoat or sacrificial lamb, as in archaic cultures, but we may sacrifice our individual needs or desires out of solidarity or love so that others can live well. Of course, when we do that, we hope that we are not just sacrificing but getting something out of it as well, that's clear. But the thought that life is a kind of sacrifice as well is not so far-fetched. You gave the example of Viktor Springer in the war, who took your place, in a sense, maybe not with much reflection but out of a feeling: there are young people here who are in great danger and I have already lived a part of my life. Better that I should be shot by the soldiers rather than them.

DSR: Of course, but I do not know whether one should impute that reasoning to him.

JK: I do not know either, I simply wanted to clarify this idea of sacrifice using an example.

DSR: The idea of sacrifice is an interpretation; it is externally brought to bear on an event. A guest looks at the parents giving the children all the cherries and only pretending to eat some themselves. The children eat all the cherries and the guest thinks, "How kind of the parents to sacrifice their own enjoyment of these delicious cherries for that of the children." But for the parent it is an even greater joy, and there is no question of their suffering by it—what we would consider the definitive quality of a sacrifice. In a situation of true sacrifice, the one sacrificing will answer life joyfully and give life whatever it is currently demanding. If life now demands that I give my life in order for others to live—the Bodhisattva idea—then I will do so joyfully.

JK: We know that Jesus grappled with his knowledge in the garden of Gethsemane, in the sense that he knew that this betrayal to the point of trial—for questioning religious authorities, thus tipping the religious system into a crisis and undermining the powerful—would inevitably lead to his death under the circumstances of the time. And Jesus as a human being had to grapple with this knowledge.

DSR: And as a human being, he does so with joy. Joy is something other than happiness—here is the greatest unhappiness he can encounter, but he takes it upon himself with love. In other words, he says yes to belonging with those for whom he is standing in, for this little community, for the idea of God's reign. He says this yes in joy, and is nevertheless despondent at how much it will cost him at the same time. But he still says it with joy.

JK: And simultaneously, the human side of this decision is made clear when, for example, Jesus says on the cross, "My God, My God, why have you forsaken me?" Jesus does not die with a smile on his lips, as has been said of Buddha, as far as is recorded, but with a scream.

DSR: The Christian tradition underscores clearly the extent to which suffering is part of the Great Mystery of God. In India, I have seen this somewhat kitschy picture of Christ on the Mount of Olives in the moonlight. It is very widespread and stands on the home altars of many families. They call him the suffering God, which is an image that is otherwise missing from the Hindu pantheon. It is an achievement of the Christian tradition to integrate suffering into the encounter with God in this way.

JK: In the sense that it is not about suffering itself, but suffering is a reality of life. To stay in biblical imagery, it is a consequence of the fall from Grace, the banishment from Paradise. Living also means suffering—being confronted with ephemeralness, with limits, with illness and death—and yet not being left alone in those, not needing to be perfect and still being redeemed. It is precisely the imperfect, the incomplete, the not-yet-whole that is redeemed.

DSR: But suffering is not the last word. It is the painful fracture of the temporal and bodily, and a departure into what goes beyond. Eichendorff put it so well:

> Now suffering, a secret
> and silent thief, creeps near;
> we all must face departure
> from all that we hold dear.
>
> If You reigned not in heaven
> what would be left on earth?
> Who could stand all the clamor?
> Who then would wish for birth?

And then the most important stanza:

> You gently break above us
> our castles in the air
> that we may see the heavens—
> so I shall not despair.[8]

This gaze up to heaven to see something that extends beyond suffering—that is what it is about.

JK: Together with Swami Satshidananda and Rabbi Joseph Gelberman, you founded the *Center for Spiritual Studies* in the United States. In connection with the Center and the House of Prayer movement, you encountered a hunger for spiritual experience in the Western Christian tradition. What does the Christian tradition need today to become more alive and to better understand the treasures it contains?

DSR: After all those decades, I am still where I was at the beginning. Interfaith encounters are something that seems likely to have a long history ahead of it. There is still much that we can learn from one another.

But we should not blur our differences. It is like two styles of music: each has its own beauty. Nothing is achieved by mixing them.

JK: But one must learn to understand one through the other.

DSR: I would go even further. I would say that each of the different spiritual traditions has its strengths but also its weaknesses. Sometimes we can recognize a weakness in our own tradition by comparison with other traditions. The other might express an insight of human religiousness better, for example. In this sense, interfaith dialogue can be very helpful, but it needs to be held by practitioners, not theoreticians.

JK: What are you thinking of when you say "practitioner"?

DSR: Of the fact that between the various institutions of religion there can at best be a kind of gentleman's agreement. Institutions do have their justification; they are necessary, but as institutions, they are first and foremost concerned with ensuring their own survival. Monks, on the other hand, are interested in spirituality. They do not need to defend an institution. That is why interfaith dialogue is typically carried out by monks or by people who have cultivated their inner monk. I call those people "practitioners." Practical experience, not interpretation, is the decisive factor.

JK: In a globalized world, but also in a world characterized by violent outbreaks, the religions have a great duty: at least of working toward peace and justice by any means possible. But we can see that that is only just a beginning. At the Parliament of World Religions in 1993, Hans Küng made an initial attempt with his "World Ethic Project." Now, however, critics of his approach point out that religion cannot simply be reduced to ethical principles, and religions feel misrepresented. What would be your approach for how religions, whose claims to truth do hold the potential for violence, can work toward peace for their adherents? What insights should religions put forward as institutions? What should they support?

DSR: One thing that all religions share, and that can also connect them deeply, if emphasized, is gratitude. Gratitude is very close to love, since love consists of saying yes to mutual belonging, and gratitude consists of continuously saying yes to life. I am talking about a joyous, celebratory yes. Each spiritual tradition praises gratefulness and professes that gratitude is its deepest concern. If the religions make good on that claim and consciously cultivate grateful living, they are simultaneously demonstrating their commonality.

JK: But would this gratitude also protect religions from jealousy, covetousness, and claims to sole truth and power? It that enough? We also see that some religious groups like to point out cultural, intellectual, and religious differences. So, for example, one might say, "The West is decadent, liberal, and devoid of values. Simply put, it is godless."

DSR: And simply put, that is correct.

JK: Is that true?

DSR: Yes, unfortunately it is.

JK: People believe in something.

DSR: We first need to recognize that, honestly recognize it and reform our own position, otherwise we are in the wrong. Every step toward our own improvement also brings us closer to mutual understanding. We could start by respecting human rights more ourselves.

JK: Human rights began as a process of progress in European history, which had been shaped and shaken so strongly by religious wars. The insight was that the primary justification of human rights should not be made religiously, about God, since that would carry the danger of rival religious truth claims and thus potentially lead to further conflict. This premise gave rise to the attempt to establish some form of separation between church and state, ensuring the freedom of religion. In Western democracies, one is therefore allowed to believe and say anything, but no religion may raise itself up to claim, "It is thus and *only thus. Only we* are right." Within a pluralistic framework, such a totalitarian claim to truth would be a potential source of conflict. To that extent, this construction of a secular state is a form of progress, not an expression of godlessness. And yes, in Europe, we speak of God less quickly in political contexts than is conventional in, say, the United States, which has a completely different history. That has advantages and disadvantages. It can have the disadvantage of cutting God out of the discussion and even forgetting about God. In today's Europe, I see that as a clear given. But on the other hand, it has the advantage of not instrumentalizing God for all too human purposes.

DSR: Yes, that is an advantage.

JK: You said earlier that on the surface, the diagnosis of decadence was correct. But there is a deeper dimension that you did not speak about. In this sense, it might be a misinterpretation, because, in fact, there are a great many important values lived in our society, even if it no longer considers itself religious because of breaks with tradition.

DSR: I suggest that we first take this critical diagnosis to heart and not be so quick to point to human rights as an achievement. There are many tasks even in that context that we first still need to solve. On the other side, those who raise this charge of decadence, themselves have the task of upholding human rights that are not seldom violated in the name of God. Both sides have a duty to be self-critical.

JK: Now this I don't quite understand. We are convinced that human rights are universally applicable. Now, Hans Küng even starts from the premise that the fundamental values formulated in human rights are espoused, lived, or at least aimed at in all traditions—independent of their different justifications in the traditions. It is precisely that premise that I am attempting to strengthen.

DSR: Yes, strengthening that is certainly important in interfaith dialogue. That is another good example of how, when we encounter other traditions, we generally see that we recognize common things. All traditions fundamentally recognize human rights, with different emphases.

If we made human rights the topic of discussion, it could become one of the most important aspects of interfaith dialogue. That is why it is no coincidence that Hans Küng introduced them at the Parliament of World Religions in Chicago. I am happy that I could be a signatory to that original document.

JK: But your previous piece of advice was that practitioners rather than the institutions should enter into dialogue. To this is added the problem that in many major religions, there are no spokes-people whom everyone recognizes. Who can speak for all Muslims, all Hindus, all Buddhists?

DSR: The dialogue, in truth, would need to be held between individuals. We should make an effort to know those of other faiths or create discussion groups whose members come from different cultures and religions. There are efforts to support and animate such groups, and that seems to me something that is very important. One does not need to talk about religion. It may be better simply to celebrate and fast together. Could Christians not fast together with Muslims? Ramadan would offer a wonderful opportunity. Christians could invite those of other faiths for Christmas, celebrate with them. This is the primary level on which encounters between religions should occur.

With Swami Satchidananda

With Sri Chinmoy and Mother Teresa; Spiritual Summit,
United Nations Headquarters, New York, October 24, 1975

With His Holiness Dalai Lama; MIT Boston, November 2014

6

A HERMIT'S LIFE

1976–1986

In the sixth decade of my life, the fact that I was permitted to live in the New Camaldoli Hermitage at Big Sur on the California coast would become highly significant. The community at New Camaldoli combines elements of communal life and hermit life. As already mentioned, I was invited there and received as a brother. For fourteen years, New Calmadoli became my monastic home in between my many travels.

There I also learned, to my astonishment, that a thousand years ago, St. Romuald, the founder of the Camaldolese branch of the Benedictine order, had developed a model for monastic life that is proving especially relevant in our time. Our life expectancy has grown so much that a young person who enters a monastery today can expect to be a monk for two or even three times as long as someone in Benedict's time. While monastic vows hold for an entire life, putting them into practice in one and the same form for so many decades can seem monotonous. In addition to conventional communal life, the Camaldolese model also offers two additional forms. The first is known as mission, and encompasses any form of service for which a monk may be sent outside of the monastery: teaching, artistic endeavors, caring for the old or sick, helping the addicted, street ministry, or spiritual counsel in prisons. The second alternative to communal life in a monastery is life as a hermit. Monks can therefore live their vows switching between these three forms—hermitage, monastic community, or social service. Thomas Merton was among those who considered this a promising and visionary model for monastic life. I had begun to practice it in my own life, long before I had heard of it.

My many travels and my times as a hermit are closely connected: from early on, my life has pulsated in the tension between the two relational poles of inward and outward contact. Even a hermit who understands his task does not merely refrain from outward contact, as such. And for what goal? To renew that same inward connectedness without which any outward contact must remain superficial. A short fable illustrates that well: Every year, a hermit retreated deeper into his cave. Mockingly, a visitor asked him, "What do you expect to find in the deepest depths of your cave?" And the hermit answered, "All the world's tears."[1]

All of us need both breadth and depth—travels outward into the breadth of the wide world, and retreats into our inward depth. The rhythm and shape of these alternating desires differ from person to person. For me, times dedicated to inwardness are vital. That, like so many things, is both a need and a gift—and as a gift, it is both blessing and duty. Even as a child, I would constantly look for and discover places to be alone. One of my favorite places was an isolated wellspring. I never tired of sitting there all on my own and listening to the water. As a student, I would sometimes flee from a party in full swing (as much as I loved to dance!) to the only place where I could be alone: the bathroom. In my summer on the Alm, finding a place to look inward amidst the postwar chaos was just as important to me as the fact that I got something to eat there. As a young monk, too, I was sometimes permitted to spend a day or even several days at the small hermit's cabin in the monastery woods. That began as the result of a dream in which something (I could not name it) weighed heavily on me. Desperately, I would search for a way out, and finally a long, narrow tunnel led me into the open. There I stood, in brilliant sunlight, and looking around, saw our hermitage. We had called it *Porta Coeli*—"Heaven's Gate"—and that is indeed what it became for me: the place of a blessedness that cannot be put into words.

Later, when I began to go on lecture tours, periods of aloneness became more important than ever. Fellow brothers often do not look kindly on this need. The typical response is "If a brother is strong enough to live on his own, we need him in our community. If he is not, then he needs us." But my abbot told me, "You are among so many people outside. When you return home, you do not need more people, not even your fellow brothers in the monastery. The hermitage will be good for you." He was right. At first, I would retreat to one or the other of our hermitages at Mount Saviour, then eventually to other fitting locations. Some of them—I will describe a few in greater detail later—were quite romantic, such as Bear Island, a tiny island in the North Atlantic where I was grateful to survive a winter of record-breaking cold, or Sand Island Light, an abandoned lighthouse on the Gulf of Mexico from where I could see nothing but sea and sky. But one should not have any romantic ideas about the life of a hermit. In the end, it requires sober confrontation with oneself and with "all the tears of the world." Part of the hermit's life includes being willingly "exposed on the cliffs of the heart," as Rilke has poetically put it.[2] The outward expression of being inwardly exposed and making oneself vulnerable to oneself is the surrender of bourgeois complacency.

I had the opportunity of experiencing that on Bear Island, a tiny isle of about seven hectares, which has space only for a coast guard lighthouse and the hundred-year-old summer home of the Dunbar family.[3] These generous friends gave me the permission to house myself in one of their buildings. I selected a wooden structure with a workshop and wood storage space on the ground level and two rooms above. Rick Dunn, who was my loyal helper there in the winter of 1976/77, helped me insulate the rooms from the winter elements. In the middle ages, St. Francis of Assisi had called for a hermit brother to always have a second as a companion; we find this practice as far back as the early desert fathers. When that cooperation is successful, it grants the hermit greater outward and inward freedom. In our case, it succeeded, as Rick mastered the art of brotherly care and the even rarer art of making himself invisible precisely out of care.

We managed to keep ourselves warm quite well with our wood stoves; on the wall's top shelf it was even warm enough for several seedlings to sprout. But the wind would blow in a little pile of snow through a hole in the wall, which was after all not entirely winter-proof. There was a great deal of wind, and during the strongest storm of that winter, we had to flee to the lighthouse in the middle of the night. The lighthouse—by permission of "Captain," the cat—housed Steve Cancellari of the Coast Guard; his wife, Mary; and their daughter, Maggie, as well as their infant. We would normally see them only on Sundays when all of us would go to Southwest Harbor for mass in the same motorboat. That could become quite dangerous even in the boat, as it did on Christmas Day. When we set out, the sea was as smooth as glass, but after the service, the waves were so high that Steve would not attempt the crossing back until hours later. And it was a daring attempt: Rick and I could hardly bail the water out of the boat fast enough to keep up with the waves pouring over the side, while Mary tried to calm the crying children. Despite all his skill, Steve was unable to maneuver the boat to the correct place at the dock, so that we had to carry the children ashore through waist-deep water cold as ice. We celebrated the rest of Christmas Day in bed, with what little alcoholic beverages we could find.

And if motorized crossings could get dangerous, they were nothing compared to the rowing. More than once, we thought our last hour had come. But this kind of "sweet danger, ripening" is part of life as a hermit as well.[4]

I got to experience a very different facet of life in the high desert of New Mexico. The monks of Mount Saviour had already founded the Monastery of Christ in the Desert there under Father Aelred Wall in 1964. I was privileged to experience Lent on my own in an adobe hut not far from the monastery. Over that period, the joint celebration with the brothers became a source of strength for my time alone because there the Hours were dictated by the cosmic rhythm of days and seasons, as Benedict had intended. Walking to prayer through the desert, under the night sky hung with stars like glittering dewdrops, hearing the coyotes howl around me—that was an incomparable beginning to the day. Then, depending on the position of the sun, different brown, red, violet, orange stone walls of the canyon would be illuminated during each hour of the day, until—after the last flare of sunset—dusk muted and faded the interplay of color. This hourly transformation of the light gave the days an outward and inward order.

A hermit monk is not supposed to decide on a fixed rhythm of the days (those who want that have communal life). He is supposed to remain free to be led by the Spirit, which "blows where it chooses" (John 3:8). But this divine breath of life is expressed in the rhythm of the cosmos, so that rhythm will naturally shape the daily rhythm in the hermitage, however it might otherwise look in the details. The more we inwardly adapt to nature, the more we become capable of resisting the arbitrariness that is so prominent in our society. I became particularly aware of this aspect of hermit life in those weeks that I spent—as foreshadowed by the name of the monastery—with Christ in the desert.

I experienced yet another form of hermitage during my days on Sand Island—an island in the Gulf of Mexico that is just large enough to fit a lighthouse. The lighthouse is 130 feet high, and if toppled, would extend far beyond the island itself. We—I was with my friend, Franciscan Father Augustin Gordon—had to search a long time before we found a fisherman who was willing to bring us the eighteen miles from Mobile, Alabama, to that forlorn dot out in the great blue. In the end, we did find one who was willing, and he promised also to pick us back up at an agreed-upon day. Despite the high waves, he brought us close enough that we could throw our backpacks on land and jump after them; there was neither a dock, nor (despite the island's name) even a grain of sand, only forbidding stone cliffs. The lighthouse keeper's hut had burned down long ago, and the sea had swallowed its remains. All that was still standing was the lighthouse itself, and we had to climb up its outside to get to the door, which had apparently once led from the hut's second floor into the lighthouse. The spiral staircase was still in quite good condition, so we were able to get up into the lamp room, where we spread out our sleeping bags. We would meet daily to celebrate the Eucharist together; the rest of the time we spent separately on the balcony that circled the tower below its highest peak—each of us silent and looking out at sky and sea. As we beheld this distance, more and more "inner world-space" opened around us, and aloneness turned into all-one-ness.

In most cases, the places where I lived alone were far less extraordinary—though all of them became very dear to me. One remains especially dear: the hermitage that I had the honor of establishing with my friend Father John Giuliani. Together, we participated in the founding of Benedictine Grange in Connecticut. We called our experiment the Grange because the word described not only a small monastic enclave away from the monastery but also a storage space for grain; the eremitic life is part of the grain of monasticism to be stored for the future. For that reason, I had the privilege of settling in one half of our little garage and even building a second floor, though that turned out to be so low that one could not stand upright in it. The British poet Kathleen Raine visited me, climbed up the ladder, carefully kept her head bowed, and sat down at the desk.[5] Later, she dedicated a poem to me on the question of how many angels could dance on the head of a pin. I did feel surrounded by angels at all times, but too dramatic an outward environment can become a distraction to the hermit's project. In almost any environment, the essential aspect should be successful: being alone with the All-One—*solus cum Solo*—in a daily rhythm without arbitrary demands, "exposed" and open to "all the world's tears."[6]

Finally, there is a hermitage where I felt particularly at home: Sky Farm Hermitage. My friend Father Dunstan Morrissey, OSB, had been gifted a large piece of land in Sonoma, California, north of San Francisco, where he would retreat to his sky farm. The name might have been suggested by the fact that during the day there is not much to harvest there, while at night the black sky curves overhead like a tree heavy with the ripe fruits of stars so close you could touch them. For years, my friends Sister Michaela and Brother Francis had been looking for the right place to realize the kind of hermitage they had been imagining. As I was visiting them, we spoke about their plans and hopes, and without further ado, I wrote to Father Dunstan: "The two of us are getting older. What do you think of the idea that Michaela and Francis might help you out as you age and then continue running Sky Farm?" By one of those rare coincidences, the postman who took my letter also brought a card from Father Dunstan to Brother Francis: "Would you send me Br. David's address? I seem to have misplaced it, and I want to give him Sky Farm." As quickly as possible, the three of us visited Father Dunstan, and a month later, he had signed Sky Farm over to us.

Here was the first place I experienced hermitage as a "home": while I could spend my time at Sky Farm only when I was not traveling, I knew that it was where I belonged. We did not own the land and the hermitages built on it, but we did hold them in trust and were responsible for this little paradise. We planted trees—olive trees that may give shade and fruit to other hermits there in a hundred years. Land where one may plant trees gives the heart a home.

In their own way, the pillar-saints, or stylites, of the first millennium AD, who did not venture down from their pillars for years, must have felt this joy of at-home-ness. And since their pillars would daily attract pilgrims and seekers, the joy of sharing must have been added as well. At Sky Farm, we too shared this joy. There were three spaces available for guests, and they were nearly always occupied. Two of them were huge vats donated by a vineyard. All that one needed for days of retreat fit comfortably in their spacious interiors. Just as we all carry the monk within us as an archetype, we also carry the hermit. Our greatest joy at Sky Farm was being able to share this gift with others who wanted to encounter their inner hermit, even if only for a short time. After all, is not all of life merely borrowed time?

DIALOGUE

JK: The Camaldolese monks with whom you spent fourteen years at Big Sur have three forms of monastic calling: hermitage, monastic community, and social service. In your case, over the course of your life, that calling has taken on all three forms. You were and are a spiritual teacher and travel a great deal. But there are also periods of contemplative life in community and periods of eremitic life. You have said that in hermitage, a monk is "exposed on the cliffs of the heart" and must find "all the world's tears," or at least leave his heart open to them. What specifically do you mean by that?

DSR: That a hermit is not avoiding life. That was what I meant in that context. And that eremitic life is not fleeing from community. Eremitic life gives those who practice it correctly a deep community with everyone and especially with those who are suffering.

I Am Because of You

JK: How does it do that? What does it mean that "the world's tears" are with me in the cave, or the hut, or whatever form the hermitage takes?

DSR: Being alone and meditating make us more sensitive and strengthen our compassion for people, animals, and all of creation.

JK: But in a hermitage, how do I encounter all that? How does that work?

DSR: From within, by way of meditation—simply because one is not distracted and does not let oneself become distracted. The world is full of tears. Virgil wrote, *"Sunt lacrimae rerum et mentem mortalia tangunt"* (All things are of tears, and what is to die touches our soul). Most of the time, we are not aware of that, and prefer to let ourselves be distracted from it. That is why it is difficult to live alone: one has nowhere to escape. One could say one is naked to all confrontation, and to all the world's suffering as well.

JK: It is said of biblical prophets all the way up to Jesus but also of the early monks in the Scetis that they often had their key experiences in the desert.[7] You also spent time repeatedly in the deserts of New Mexico where one is confronted with an emptiness and with oneself. In the face of such experiences, either one gives up or one grows inwardly. What did your desert experiences confront you with, and what did you find there?

DSR: Any person who goes into the desert will probably experience that there are, as we said, no distractions there. One is confronted with nature in its sheer size, its overwhelming beauty, for example, of the starry night sky. In the desert, one can see the stars so much more clearly. They appear so large. But in the desert, we also confront the roughness of nature, for example, in the cold chill of night.

JK: One is also much more grateful for the resources one has available, even if it is only the water necessary for survival.

DSR: Yes, one grows more grateful for all things. And if one lets oneself be affected by that instead of escaping into distraction or simply going away, that gratitude leads to an inward deepening.

JK: Were there any moments in which you thought, "Why am I doing this to myself? I'm in the wrong place!" Are there those moments as well?

DSR: I cannot really remember any. I was always very happy to be alone. The only time I ever felt that I did not belong was not in a hermitage but sometimes in large crowds. Even though it happens only rarely, I feel out of place there—for example, at receptions, where there are many people and superficial conversations. For me, this experience is like wasted time, but aloneness is different; that is never wasted. It was not always easy, but I always knew that this is where I belong.

JK: What interests me is the psychodynamics in the moment in which I no longer have any distractions around me, where no one is talking to me, where I am relying completely on myself for survival. What is so primeval about this experience?

DSR: Perhaps something like: things become more still, like water becoming still. It grows clear and one can see deeper and deeper. One can breathe more deeply, and something like a cosmic empathy begins to set in. One feels a connection with all things.

JK: One is also in resonance with one's surroundings, the time of day, perhaps with the few animals one sees in the desert?

DSR: Yes. When one has no one else in the hermitage other than a fly, one feels a very personal relationship with it. I have also heard of Irish hermits who had friendly relationships with their mice.

JK: And fed them?

DSR: Yes.

JK: Can you describe a typical day for you in the hermitage?

DSR: That was very varied. A very important point is that hermits do not set a fixed daily schedule for themselves. That does not mean that one sleeps as long as one wants to every day. There are certain monastic norms. But most of all, life with a natural daily rhythm is highly important. One can consciously experience sunrise and dawn. One feels noon when everything grows still. One is filled with joy at the cooling of late afternoon and when evening falls. One becomes far more conscious of the natural course of the day. Compared with nature, the normal course of the day in the city is quite arbitrary; it does not matter whether it is getting dark, because one can simply turn on the light and prolong the day as much as one wants to. During very short winter days in the hermitage, I did use light as well, but otherwise I normally preferred to live in the rhythm of normal daylight. In winter, one sleeps longer than in the summer. Originally, that was also the case with the monks living in communal monasteries. For example, Benedict writes very specifically that dinner should be held at such a time that everything is finished before it is dark. It is important to accept the natural course of the day. In comparison, it is then much less important how one fills the day; when one writes, or reads, or does handiwork.

JK: Did different projects lead you into hermitage?

DSR: There have been times when I have retreated to work on a book project, but I would not describe that as eremitic life. The hermit's only project is being alone and free. Other projects get in the way of that endeavor. Being alone with the All-One, as Plotinus has said, this aloneness in and of itself is the project.

JK: And that is different from loneliness.

DSR: Being alone can take positive and negative forms. We refer to the negative form as being lonely. We are lonely when we are cut off from others, and being cut off is the negative thing. We can also be lonely in the center of a crowded room. All that it means is that we are not connected with the others; we feel inwardly cut off. We do not actually have a proper term for the positive form of aloneness.

JK: Perhaps autonomy?

DSR: No, that sounds far too willful. The hermit's vulnerability is part of aloneness. Admittedly, that is not something one usually thinks of.

It may not be that important to find the precise term for it; at any rate, a lonely person is cut off from community with others while the hermit is deeply connected with them. And the deeper and more encompassing this inner connection, the more authentic—and happy—eremitic life will be. Our greatest happiness, our truest joy, is connection with others. Our greatest sorrow is to be cut off from them.

JK: You mentioned a hermit's vulnerability just now. How is a hermit vulnerable?

DSR: In confrontation with himself. Distraction is like an armor we can put on to avoid feeling this vulnerability. Why would someone want to make themselves vulnerable? Because in the end, it is our authentic state: we are vulnerable. One has to admit that before one can be open with others in a true relationship. Those who are open to relationships are also open to injury.

JK: But at least in that moment, the hermit does not have this relationship with other people.

DSR: Yes, he does! Not only with other people, but with every-thing there is. This vulnerability is not only and not even primarily about the insults to which one is exposed, but about the small-ness one experiences standing under the starry sky of the desert, the insignificance one feels there: I am nothing.

JK: But that could also lead me to humility. It does not need to be an injury. Vulnerability, wounding—I sense that that is something stronger and has to do with our darker side.

DSR: What I meant by vulnerability comes very close to humility: not putting on any kind of armor.

JK: Could one call that sensitivity, a special kind of awareness?

DSR: Yes. Sensitivity, awareness, compassion—meaning shared joy and shared suffering. The *shared* part is the deciding factor. Not cutting off but connecting.

JK: I would like to get back to the darker sides with which we are confronted, so please bear with me for a moment.

People are creatures of infinite want. Though most aren't conscious of this, human hunger is marked by its longing for the absolute. However, anyone who tries to still this infinite longing by finite means, making it dependent solely on successful life cir-cumstances, will have little reason for joy in life. On the contrary, there is a high likelihood that longing will slide into addiction—addictive actions or stimulants will then briefly enable a feeling of connection or lift the fear of disconnectedness. Translating the Latin root word *religare* as "to reconnect," religion then becomes a different name for connectedness. But back to addictions: they come in many forms, beginning with the addiction to work, which many see as harmless and some praise highly. But there is also addiction to power, sex, gambling, alcohol, or drugs. Especially in addiction, one feels an unfreedom. What is interesting is that the Egyptian monks of the Scetis knew this already. In the doctrine of the eight temptations, they called it "the demonic." One is, so to speak, no longer in charge of one's own house. As the Viennese say about someone who is no longer in full possession of their own faculties, "It got him." Do you as a hermit also know such conflicts with addictiveness?

DSR: I had never seen it from that point of view. I would express it like this: as a hermit, the end goal is to be in the present moment, the desert fathers showed early on that there are only three fundamental ways of missing that goal. The first is to hold on to things that are ephemeral and may have passed already, but we are still holding on to them—some kinds of desires, lust, or something similar—and that is always a danger. When one does not have much, one holds on to what little one has. That clinging always remains the same, no matter whether it is clinging to fantasies or memories. There is a great deal of opportunity for that in the life of a hermit. So, holding on to things holds one up: one is not in the moment but belongs to the past.

The second way is anger. The bad part of anger is its impatience. Anger in and of itself is a strong burst of energy, and its impatience is the only bad thing about it: one wants to force a certain kind of future and thus fails to live in the present moment. One would think that this has exhausted all the options, but we are quite creative when it comes to this.

The third possibility is that one is neither holding on to the past nor reaching for the future, but instead asleep in the present, or not awake. But being in the present moment, being alive in it, means being awake to it, and this has nothing to do with our sleep during the night. On the contrary. The Song of Solomon, for example, expresses it like this: "I slept, but my heart was awake" (5:2). There is a waking sleep, a praying sleep. It is not hard to experience it. But before, I was talking of a different sleep, which the desert fathers called the "Noonday Demon." At midday, when it is hottest in the desert, one tends to doze off and is not truly present. That is a danger when one is alone, because no one comes to wake one up. This spiritual and intellectual dozing is a great danger. It is another way in which one can fail to be truly awake to the moment. In addition, being awake means being awake to the suffering of the world, to the fact that someone is dying and someone is being born every instant. We do not normally have the time to think of that, much less feel it or be actively conscious of it. But in a hermitage, one has nothing more important to do.

JK: What you have just described, the "Noonday Demon," was what Evagrius Ponticus described as *acedia*, "spiritual listlessness." Evagrius considered this to be the monk's greatest danger, becoming spiritually discouraged and listless. Bland, one would say. One has no taste for life anymore and does not know what to do with oneself and the world. That may also be a subtle form of depression.

DSR: Or of midlife crisis. A midlife crisis is something like acedia.

JK: How do I fight that, or rather, how do I prevent spiritual listlessness from taking hold of me? What are the countermeasures to become awake again, or even stay awake?

DSR: Not subjecting oneself to a fixed schedule in the hermitage is part of it. When I realize that I am starting to doze, it is time to do something that gives me joy, whether or not my plan for the day had accounted for that. It sounds funny, but it is important to keep on the lookout for things that give one joy and to do those things that give one joy.

JK: Can you give an example of something that has given you joy?

DSR: Chopping wood is one example. If I have planned to read for an hour but begin to doze after a quarter of an hour, I can go outside and chop firewood. That gives me joy and awakens me. I can also take a brief walk; that is also part of my life in hermitage. In those cases, it is often good to do something that is long overdue because one has kept delaying it out of laziness. Acedia is actually laziness. One already has enough to do if one simply tries to remain awake to each moment over the course of the day.

JK: Your time on the small islands must have been especially challenging. Sand Island, for instance, is a pile of rocks, and on them an abandoned lighthouse. You and a fellow brother had to have yourselves brought there by boat. How can one do that, two people being alone in the same place?

DSR: In this case, there was enough space on Sand Island to spend the entire day alone on two different sides of the balcony without even seeing one another. Then we would celebrate the Eucharist together. But we would eat alone again. The Eucharist was our time of community.

JK: Though there are few classical hermits today, that way of life does seem to be very attractive: retreating to an isolated mountaintop hut, living in the wilderness in a tent or under a tarp, exposed to the elements—plenty of individuals keep looking for that. There are also new offers that take up old spiritual traditions such as the vision quest, initiation rites, and so on. What, in your opinion, are these people looking for or finding?

DSR: I believe that they are looking for and—when successful—finding exactly what other hermits search for and find. Today, there are few hermits who live their entire lives as hermits, and maybe there never were very many. But temporary hermitage has almost become a necessity for many people, especially in our society. Some go hiking on their own, others have a hut or a dwelling where they stay, and there are also monasteries that make hermitages available for a time. Conscious solitude probably always has religious overtones, whether it occurs in a monastic environment or during a hike through the mountains. As human beings, aloneness is always an opportunity for encountering the Great Mystery. Sustaining that aloneness for an entire life is indeed something quite unusual. I can imagine that it would really be something like a profession. For me, in any case, it was not.

JK: You needed the rhythm, the dynamics of aloneness, community, and being able to work with people?

DSR: Yes. Many people today—and not just monks—find that they can serve their community best if they intermittently retreat, collect themselves, and find themselves. They have more to give that way.

JK: Sometimes one also develops a very clear view of the circumstances in which one is living. Like Henry David Thoreau, who developed his criticism of American society in the nineteenth century when he was living as a hermit.[8] That was powerful, and it became a foundational text, one of the many foundational texts of the hippie movement in the late 1960s.

DSR: I myself once made a pilgrimage to Walden Pond, where Thoreau lived as a hermit for a time. Unfortunately, his hut is no longer standing.

JK: And how was that?

DSR: Touching. His spirit is still there.

JK: He was, in the best sense, an incredibly archaic thinker.

DSR: In fact, he was imprisoned briefly. My first visit to Walden Pond happened to coincide—if there are such things as coincidences—with Earth Day.

7

ENCOUNTERS IN TRAVEL

1986–1996

Though my long lecture tours started only in the seventh decade of my life, I enjoyed traveling even in my youth. We called it "going on a ride"—tramping for days, even weeks, with our heavy backpacks. Because my birthday was during the summer holidays, I could never celebrate this day with my mother. Her response was always, "Well, you're my little gypsy."

Leaving and breaking off all ties with the home was a way of articulating our independence, and independence was important to us. I still marvel at how generously my mother allowed me that independence and even encouraged it. How difficult it must have been for her! On a ride, my brothers and I were no less cut off and unreachable than Scott and Amundsen at the South Pole. In an emergency, we would probably have been able to telephone, even half a century before cell phones, but fortunately, no emergency ever occurred; and so, from departing hug to joyful welcome greeting weeks later, my mother knew nothing of us or our whereabouts.

A typical "ride"—we are traveling to the Bohemian Forest—starts by train. The train ride itself is an adventure, particularly on the little local train we change to in Regensburg. It is libelously claimed that the tracks of this line do not run exactly parallel, and so the wheels are not fully screwed on, in order that the train can adjust to the changing gauges. Certainly, that is what it feels like when the train rattles and sways into motion. If I remember correctly, the little village where we get off and start our hiking is called Zwiesel. "Going on a ride" is actually illegal—unless it is as part of the Hitler Youth—but no one but us is hiking here, and we feel safe. In any case, we keep secret anything having to do with our rides. Most of the time, we come here with sworn friends from the *Neulandschule*, but this time it is just my two brothers and me. Max is thirteen, Hans is fourteen, and I am sixteen. It is not long until we are engulfed by the forest. For days, we wander through practically unending bushes of blueberries. We carry hardly any food in our packs, and the berries are our main source of nourishment. Only once or twice a day do we pass a house, a forester's or charcoal burner's hut. Then we send in Maxi to ask for directions. Admittedly, we have a map, but we also have ulterior motives: "If they give you something to drink," we tell our youngest brother, who looks hungry, "you can drink it, but if they give you bread, you must put it in your pocket and share with us." Our method proves highly successful.

Through the forest, we come to the barren loneliness of the high moors, then to the mountains. One of them is called the Arber. Just below its peak—as with other mountains close by—there is a small mountain lake. Bathing in that icy water is a test of our courage. At night, we sleep in tents. If our group is larger, four of us carry one side each of the *Kohte*, which when assembled in the evening can sleep up to a dozen of us.[1] Inside, we can build a fire and cook in a large pot. Then, by the light of the fire, we sit around the pot and eat directly out of it. For this reason, we carry long spoons that we call "Puszta spoons."[2] The smoke escapes through an opening in the tent, though it does also rain in through the same opening if we are not quick enough to extinguish the fire and close the smoke hatch. This time, however, it is only three of us, so a small tent is enough; we are used to sleeping in cramped quarters. On another "ride" to the Bohemian Forest, six of us once had to sleep in a forest chapel that was so small that if one of us turned over in his sleep, all the others had to as well. If the weather is good, we three brothers often sleep under the stars. When we pass villages, farmers will often let us sleep in the hayloft. We even carry an impressive letter of recommendation from our local cardinal and archbishop—which becomes important during one of our rides. I am sick, and the concerned local pastor diagnoses, "His pulse is racing!" I am allowed to sleep in a real bed in the vicarage until I am better, even with a real quilt. Then we walk on. Mother does not need to know.

One of the high points of this ride through the Bohemian Forest is our visit with our friend and *Neulandschule* comrade Rupert Steinbrenner, who lives in Winterberg. Though we arrive unannounced, Rupert's mother takes us in like family, and we feel completely at home—for once, at home with sisters. This is new to us, and we are thrilled. After all the privations of the forest, we are being spoiled, experiencing home away from home. Might we have actually had something like homesickness? We would never admit it, but there are a few tears when we depart. Until then, everything is one long celebration, a celebration of our young life, with flirtation and music. We were even greeted with music fluttering out of an open window when we first arrived: a melody from Bach's Notebook for Anna Magdalena, which the youngest girl was practicing on the piano. For the three of us, this piece remains the quintessence of our visit to Winterberg and those days of unforgettable joy in life.

We also pass through other towns: Krumau, Prachditz, Rosenberg—these are the names I remember. We go into every church, pray, and look at the statues of the saints. We gain courage from belonging to this great family of the Communion of Saints. We feel at home in the churches and curiously eye each little detail. On a hand carved wooden pew—in Prachaditz, I think—we read, "Beware of cattes not so kinde, who woo in fronte and scratch behinde!" We love such discoveries and continue to laugh about the archaic spelling for a long time. Aside from church visits and overnight stays, we never stop where there are people. Even in the big cities of Regensburg and Passau we only stop to see churches—the famous ones of which we have seen pictures. Then we wander downstream along the Danube, always as close as possible to the river, along the *Treppelweg*, where men and mules used to pull barges upstream using ropes. For us, those are marvelously unobstructed walking paths.

Suddenly, we see a steamboat not far ahead of us about to cast off. As quickly as our heavy boots allow, we run toward the boat. The men aboard laugh understandingly and wave. Maxi is the last one to reach the gangway as it is being hauled in; luckily, he does not fall in the Danube but onto the boat. We are not taken far, but we are let off the boat near where raftsmen are at work. Laughing, they accept our offer of "help," and as payment we are allowed to ride along on the rafts the next morning. In Krems, the rafts are taken apart, but we have the opportunity of buying the lifeboat. We are astonished by how little the raftsmen ask for it, but as soon as we get in, we realize that with three of us in it, the boat takes in so much water that two of us are completely occupied just bailing it out. The third steers, as well as can be managed. We are cornered worryingly by an oncoming steam boat on one side and the shore on the other. After the danger has passed, we see a small chapel on the banks and, knees still weak, we stop there to say prayers of thanks.

After spending one more night—not very dryly—on a little island overgrown by reeds, we arrive in Nussdorf, tow our skiff to land, and sit on the banks of the river. Our boat now has a sign: "Firewood, for sale." In these early war years, wood is rare, so we are able to sell our boat quickly and without a loss. Back then we experienced everything that I would later see as significant aspects of travel; independence was among them, but was never again as important as in those years in which we were first allowed to taste it.

The primary aspect of traveling was always the encounters on the way—just like those encounters on our youthful rides enriched our lives forever. Each later journey also brought the same hospitality, fun, surprises, wonder, and the unavoidable tears of homesickness and farewell. Each of these key words recalls experiences from my later travels, some of which I recount here as snapshots.

The key word of those lecture tours that led me so far out into the world is *encounter*. One of those encounters started during a course called "Spirituality for Our Times," which in the 1980s, I presented each year at the Jesuit university of St. Louis, Missouri. The larger program was called "Focus on Leadership," and many of the participants had been heads of religious orders who were now able to devote a year to furthering their spiritual education after their terms had expired. They came from Asia, Africa, Australia, and other parts of the world and often wished that the other members of their order could hear the program. Consequently, I was invited to all parts of the globe; soon receiving more invitations than I could accept.

For example, the Sisters of St. Joseph of the Sacred Heart wanted me to meet all of the over one thousand sisters of their Australian order. Even within that circumscribed location, it involved a journey of over six thousand miles, since often only two or three of the "Brown Joeys" (their nickname was based on the Australian term for baby kangaroos) were serving God with the help of others, hundreds of miles from their nearest sisters. And so, I was flown by helicopter to Turkey Creek in Australia's Northern Territory. There, I was first introduced to the chiefs of the aborigines who lived around five large fires out in the open air. Two sisters taught the children—or actually the mothers and their children, to avoid generational conflict. The government had erected a schoolhouse, the only building far and wide, where the same lesson plan was to be covered as in the city schools of Sydney. The sisters did not teach in the schoolhouse but outside, and adapted the lesson plan to the circumstances as much as possible. I will never forget the encounters with the children, who gave me drawings they had made, or with their mothers, or especially with the wise elders of the tribe. Nor will I forget the many brave sisters of the order on their lonely outposts.

I have experienced such frequent and such openhearted hospitality on my travels that it is difficult for me to pick out individual examples, but Polynesia is famous for its almost overwhelmingly heartfelt hospitality. I experienced this in Apia on Samoa, where Cardinal Pio Taofinu'u had invited me to hold a retreat for all the priests of his diocese.[3] The cardinal sat in their midst, wearing nothing but a red loin cloth, and for an entire weekend, proved to me that Samoan hospitality deserves its fame. The people of Tonga, however, are no less hospitable. I was once invited by Irish monks in New Zealand, whose monastery had a host of novices from Tonga. When guests from their homeland visited the monastery, the Tongalese brothers knew no higher rule than hospitality. The singing and dancing continued half the night, and the next day all the monastery's refrigerators were empty. The novices had used up anything that was edible or drinkable. They cited Benedict in their defense: "Guests should be received as Christ himself." "This is how we would receive Christ in Tonga," they would say, and I did not know which to admire more: the hospitality of the Tongalese brothers or the patience of the Irish ones.

In Nigeria, I was given a guest gift with such innocent determination that ever new complications ensued. A chief gave me an elephant tusk with an engraved dedication. I despaired and refused as belligerently as gratitude would allow, but I was hopelessly outmaneuvered. The huge tusk did not fit in my suitcase, and I had to tie it to the outside, wrapped in newspaper. My hopes that it might be taken away by Nigerian officials turned out to be wishful thinking. All through Munich airport, I heard outraged whispers behind me, and I pleaded with customs officers to confiscate it. But to no avail. In the end, I asked a German order of nuns to sell the ivory to benefit the poor and was relieved when I was finally rid of it. Two months later, I received the proud message that one of the sisters had succeeded in smuggling the thing into the United States under her habit. My name was engraved on it—what if she had been caught?

There were plenty of further surprises. In Kenya, several lectures I was to give were canceled at short notice. I had no idea, but Japanese friends who happened to be in Nairobi at the time learned that my schedule was free and picked me up at the airport to take me on several days of safari, with lions, zebras, giraffes, and the overwhelming view of Mount Kilimanjaro. I cannot say what amazed me more: such beauty of nature or the variety of human encounters.

In New Zealand, I had the honor of participating in a ten-day centenary pilgrimage with the Sisters of Compassion. A hundred years earlier, their founder, Marie Joseph Aubert, dedicated the order to service with the Maori, against significant resistance by whites. These Maori people were showing their gratitude: each evening, we were received at a different *marae* with impressive festivities.[4] Often we had to wait for a long time until women—only women have this right—invited us to the holy place with song. Then, young warriors performed ceremonial mimed attacks on us. Only after long speeches and response speeches, when the hosts handed us a fern leaf as a sign of peace, were we officially accepted as welcome guests. We exchanged the nose kiss, or *hongi*, with everyone from the young warriors to the last infant. By then we were simply family members, uncles and aunts, to the children. We were dined lavishly and could sleep in the long-house between the carvings of the ancestors. (The entire way there, Maori children helped me gather trash. From the north of Scotland to near the South Pole, I have been able to perform this service for the environment.)

I Am Because of You

A completely different kind of pilgrimage repeatedly astounds me in India. Father Bede Griffiths, whom I am visiting in his monastery and ashram Shantivanam, entrusts me to a Hindu priest who is a friend, and together we go on a pilgrimage through the south of India—on foot, by ox cart, and even by train. In Chidambaram, where we meet not a single non-Indian person, we participate in a highly festive *Puja* in one of India's holiest temples, where both Shiva and Vishnu are worshiped.[5] Almost more touching is the attitude of a young temple priest in the Kali temple on the city's outskirts—the humility with which he encounters the poor. When we arrive in Pondicherry, Shri Udar Pinto, one of the pioneers of the experimental international city Auroville, furrows his brow at the red mark on my forehead. I feel foreign in this French enclave and am homesick for true India. Neither here nor on any of my other journeys do I want to be a tourist, much less an anthropologist. I simply want to be a person among persons.

In Taiwan, I encounter people high up in the restricted mountain areas—a rare privilege accorded to me because I have been invited here by Maryknoll Fathers. I am fascinated by the appearance of the tall, young indigenous women, now nuns, striding like white-robed queens. In my youth, head-hunting was still practiced here. One day, an indigenous catechist with whom I became friends appears very sad. "How far you have come," he explains through our interpreter, "and now we do not even have a common language." I search for an answer. Then I remember: "But we can drink together." He likes the idea. To him, it means drinking from the same glass, cheek to cheek. The rice wine tastes like petroleum, but the ritual touches me deeply. Then my friend says solemnly, "In the old days, one did that only once in life."

Is not all life only once? Is not this entire life a journey? Is not all suffering on the road homesickness, and is not this homesickness in the end a homesickness for God, for that feeling of enduring protection in the Great Mystery?

DIALOGUE

JK: "You are my little gypsy," is something your mother apparently said to you when you once again went on an exploration to the Bohemian Forest on your own, or rather as a group. The seventh decade of your life is likewise shaped by lengthy tours for seminars and lectures all over the world. You have been invited often. The title of this phase of life is headed by the word *encounters*. When we travel and encounter someone in foreign parts, then on the surface it is at first a form of contact with something new, something strange, one might say. What were the central insights and experiences that your travels made possible?

DSR: Possibly, my most important experience was that, in moments of true encounter, we still feel a deep connection with people who, outwardly, are completely different, even in their views, culture, and way of life. There is some spark that is exchanged and we are one with each other. One example comes to mind: I was in India at the time, before Indian Airlines was even working with computers. Often one had to call to secure a connecting flight. I was stranded in Madras, the city known today as Chennai. I had an Indian Airlines ticket to Calcutta and needed a connecting ticket from there. But it was rather obvious that the man trying to sell me the ticket wanted to be bribed, which I would not do out of principle. So, I had to go there several times a day, then back the next day, and again the next. He sent a telegram, and that cost something. Then he made a phone call, and that cost something as well. Then, in the end, he wanted to sell me a suspicious connecting ticket. After all this waiting, I was already somewhat worn down, but suddenly something inside me changed and I said to him, "Imagine yourself in my shoes. If you were me and I wanted to sell you this ticket, would you buy it?" At that, he fell out of his role completely and said, "Under no circumstances. That is not a good idea. But I will help you." From that point on, everything was settled quickly. He knew exactly what he needed to do and did not ask for anymore money. And everything worked perfectly. Unfortunately, I have not managed to do that very often in my life. But for me it is always a significant experience to encounter a stranger in such a way that something shines out in both of us. When that happens, the roleplay is over and real aliveness begins to flow. Aliveness is mutual connection. Where that is missing, the best we can manage is polite theater. For me the most beautiful experiences are often when foreignness is replaced with connection.

JK: Your travels often bring you into contact with more elemental religions, such as the indigenous tradition in the United States, but also in South Africa, New Zealand, and Australia. You are trained in ethnology and religious studies—both open to and curious about the things other traditions can give us. What kinds of horizons did these religions open for you? What were you able to learn from them?

DSR: The thing that touched me most is the sense of the holiness of everyday life. The separation between the sacred and the profane is not as distinct as it is for us. People are conscious of "Mana," of the power in everything, of the Mystery. They feel the Great Mystery in everything. It is like a stronger sense of vision looking through things, that feeling for the Holy. The Holy is simultaneously fascinating and thrilling, and one encounters it even in things such as building a fire or fetching water. Carrying the water, cooking it, serving the food—all those things are activities that suddenly become Holy Acts before our eyes. In India, unfortunately, this consciousness has largely disappeared in recent decades. My memories are still of the early 1970s, and back then, all of India felt like a huge cathedral. The entire country was a holy site. Even in the cities, people at that time fulfilled many sacred actions, decorated altars, honored images of deities. Every daily action expressed great reverence. I hope that might still be the case outside the cities. I would imagine it is; there are tens of thousands of Indian villages. But in the cities, the sense of the Holy seems to have been largely lost.

JK: You described some of the places where you were welcomed, such as a South Sea island. You recalled that the feature of these societies that most stood out was hospitality. Everything is shared, even if there is little to go around. Is hospitality something that you miss in our culture? Is that something we can learn from these people?

DSR: I have also experienced a great deal of hospitality in our own culture. But the difference may be that, for us, hospitality is very selective, not just toward strangers but also toward other social circles. Most people move rather exclusively within their own class as well, and that is as far as hospitality extends. In our society, it seems obvious to me. In India, it is even clearer: in practice, they still have the caste system. Comprehensive hospitality is something that is simply more prevalent in indigenous cultures. Hospitality there is not selective; it is an essential feature. It does not matter whether you are black or white, rich or poor, or different in some other way. What matters is whether you are the stranger, the one seeking refuge. That is enough as an opportunity for hospitality.

JK: That reminds me of Jesus' words: "I was a stranger and you welcomed me" (Matt 25:35)—though mirrored in a different culture.

DSR: Yes, it is simply fundamental hospitality.

JK: Hospitality without distinctions. But sometimes cultural differences can also lead to difficult moments. You related how in Nigeria you were given an entire elephant tusk, engraved with your name, as a guest gift. You tried to resist as best you could, but out of politeness, finally had to take it, only to give it away in Europe. Hospitality can have its pitfalls as well.

DSR: Yes, and it can be painful as well. For example, I was once hosted by very poor people, and I knew how much they were spending to buy me things they would never get for themselves—and which, in fact, I don't like, such as Coca-Cola and potato chips. These generous people spent money on me and did not simply share their daily bread with me, but much more. In the end, I felt it as painful. Gratefulness can also encompass that pain.

JK: One wants to give something back and cannot.

On one of your trips to India, you also visited Bede Griffiths in his ashram Shantivanam. What did you learn about religious life from him?

DSR: I had the great good fortune to know Bede Griffiths for a long time.[6] He came to our community at Mount Saviour as early as the 1950s. I have known him practically all my monastic life and admired him for how he managed to integrate Indian religious sensibility and Christian symbolism. He combined those two wonderfully. The Mass celebrated at Shantivanam felt like an offering in a temple. He fitted himself into the Indian style and that was beautiful, for example, by wafting a camphor fire to honor God. After the transubstantiation, he waved this camphor fire around the host, instead of holding up the host, as a priest would do in the West. Being able to experience that with Father Bede was beautiful.

The acculturation of Christianity in India was really his magnanimity. It was not easy for him, but he persevered.

JK: Not easy from the side of the Church?

DSR: From the side of the Church, I believe.

JK: He understood how to enculturate the Christian.

DSR: In the truest sense of the word. He was simply convinced that religions are connected by spirituality. Spirituality was alive in him. It is one and the same Mystery that is alive in all religions. He was so enlivened by it, and so intellectually convinced as well, that expressing it in liturgy and in his own way of life was completely natural. He wore the saffron robes of the sadhus, the Indian monks. It is different when one or another little detail pops up somewhere, but with him everything was organic and fitting.

JK: You asked whether all traveling might correspond to homesickness. Normally, we feel as though it is a longing for travel—wanderlust—that drives us. What do we seek when we set out into the world?

DSR: It is true that wanderlust and homesickness are very similar, and I am sometimes not at all sure whether I have one or the other. In the end, it is the desire to penetrate deeper into the Great Mystery. That expresses itself in our inward journeys—eremitic journeys—and in our outward journeys, our major travels. They do not necessarily need to be long or lead us to famous places. I am convinced that, for many people, walking to the next village over is major travel. In fact, that can be more deserving of the term *travel* than if I venture halfway around the world by plane. It depends on the attitude, the openness for experience, and the courage to expose oneself to new things.

JK: One undertakes something, no matter whether out of homesickness or wanderlust. One moves, or something similar. One could also say, "hang on," once realizing that one can just stay in place, but that is not the case. We evidently need to go on either inward or outward journeys in some way, shape, or form.

DSR: Change is an essential part of it.

JK: *Homo viator*—man is a wanderer.

I Am Because of You

DSR: In one of his prayers to God, Rilke writes, "When I go towards you, it is with my whole life." All the movement of our lives is a journey in this sense, a journey home, if you will.[7]

JK: But the journey home also requires detours, ways out, and sometimes ways of escape even, to become truly a journey home.

Since you are familiar with the religious situation in the entire world, your assessment of it interests me. Because religion is a worldwide phenomenon, if, for example, you compare Europe with the United States, the former seems to be far more atheist than the latter. In the United States, an open and vocal commitment to religious faith and invoking religion to justify one's positions and actions is almost normal, while in Europe, about 42 percent of people see themselves as atheist or close to atheism—including many of those baptized as Christians. Nietzsche's statement that God is dead, which we have already alluded to, seems to prove true in practice. In our public spaces in Europe, an existential-practical atheism or a complete indifference to religion—an apathy— has become the rule rather than the exception. Often, being religious or believing in God is seen in one's circle of friends as a little strange, if not downright suspicious. How do you understand this? How do you interpret this mood, which may be rather unique to Europe in comparison with the rest of the world?

DSR: In the United States, we encounter a very widespread fundamentalism, and I personally do not like that religious rhetoric. I regret that, in Europe, leaving the Church has become so prevalent. It may represent a necessary inner liberation for those leaving, but it also means a loss for their children, because then the next generation no longer experiences religious belonging. That security in childhood is important, even if one leaves it again later. Children need that and enjoy it as well. But in the end, it is about human engagement with the Mystery, and nowhere are people spared that. The birth of a child; the death of one's parents, friends, or relatives; one's own death—all these are situations that are deeply religious because, in them, we are unavoidably confronted by and forced to engage with the Mystery of life. Of course, it is beautiful when, as in the indigenous cultures, the religious finds expression in everyday life, when there are forms and rituals for that. That greatly enriches and eases our lives as people.

JK: No doubt, but even your interpretation of birth and death as experiences of the Mystery, as religious experiences, would be completely denied by a "religiously unmusical" agnostic. He might say, "Brother David, birth is birth, death is death. That's the circle of life, it has nothing to do with God or Mystery. We pass life on and are at an end with our death. Our highest goal in life is to pass life on to the next generation in such a way that they treat the world well. That is why it is important that the next generation live relatively decently and think well of us. We gave them life, but there is nothing beyond that."

DSR: Someone who presents such an intellectual argument is not engaging with life, but is simply giving a rigid interpretation. Imagine a woman who would say what you have just said: "Birth is birth." If she then gives birth to a child, that is something else already—and for the father who witnesses the birth as well. Or when one is standing at the deathbed of a person one loves: that is engaging with life, and there, both the religious and the atheist formulas break down. What remains is experiencing, and that experiencing is the experiencing of the Holy: the things that both fascinate us and thrill us. That is what it is about; that is where religion is.

JK: But not for those who do not see it.

DSR: But I do not know whether there really are people who do not see that. There may be people who deny it, but is there someone who really does not experience it?

JK: Perhaps not experiencing it as wonderful, but in the sense of a profane finite life. It is always wonderful when new life comes into the world and sad when a life passes.

DSR: Presented that way, all it means is that someone does not think overly much about the Mystery of life. But that is not what matters in the end: it only matters not to actively deny it. And one can deny it with the head, but not with the heart, where one does experience it. That, at least, is how I see it.

JK: But does one experience the religious or the Holy itself, or is experiencing already an interpretation?

DSR: Naming it is of course an interpretation, but what stands behind that interpretation is lived reality. One can call it what one likes.

JK: Do you not know people who essentially say, "There is no God. Life is beautiful. Let's drink and eat, because we'll be dead tomorrow"?

DSR: I do not know many such people, but then my social contacts are selective. But a person's stated doctrine is irrelevant in our context here. In other words, when someone says, "There is no God," I try to look at the person standing behind this statement. That is the same when I encounter a fundamentalist. I try to encounter the person. The doctrine does not interest me so much. We can pretend all sorts of things to ourselves.

JK: Then what is the essential factor?

DSR: In the end, it is about letting oneself be moved by the Mystery, regardless of the terms one uses to talk about it—and that is also true for people who use the right terms, and who were raised Christian and can recite the Creed and are socialized in Christianity. If the Mystery has not taken hold of them, everything else is unimportant in the end. But I am convinced that life runs its course in such a way that encounters with the Mystery are unavoidable. At the very least, we experience death. Death confronts us with something we cannot grasp but that we can understand when it takes hold of us. The same is true with music or nature for many people. I am convinced that music and nature cause the relevant religious experiences in them. When the Mystery takes hold of us, it takes us into the space that Rilke calls the "inner world-space." And that is what is essential, not interpretive terminology.

JK: A brief question about the "inner world-space": What exactly is meant by that?

DSR: Rilke had other expressions for it as well: "inner world-space," "the open," "the inaccessible"...those are poetic terms, and one needs to allow oneself to be affected by them. Something resonates in us there, but grasping it in terms, that is impossible. In the end, it comes back to being moved.

JK: And about mutual belonging?

DSR: Being moved by the Great Mystery is the experience of boundless mutual belonging. Of course, one can cultivate one's consciousness of this belonging and let it flow into one's whole life. But one can also repress it completely. One always hears that, for example, National Socialist officials such as Himmler, Göring, and Bormann were great lovers of music, and I do not want to deny that they were very moved by it. In that, they touched on the Mystery.

JK: And nevertheless, cut themselves off?

DSR: And then shut themselves off from others. That is the great danger of ideology. Ideology says, Jews must be exterminated. But the more I let myself be moved by the Great Mystery, the harder it will be for me to live by such principles. That is what I mean when I say that we can cultivate this encounter with the Mystery, support it, and bring it to our consciousness again and again. All of that is not a private matter, it belongs to a whole tradition of people who have done the same thing, who have spoken and written about it. We connect with an entire culture.

JK: The world over, as one can see when traveling.

Traveling with Anthony Chavez

8

CONTEMPLATION AND REVOLUTION

1996–2006

The more I encountered different people on my travels and the more I listened to their concerns, the more I began to suspect that a sea change in the history of the world was approaching. All the most memorable encounters centered around tears, but also around inextinguishable hope. It was especially a conversation I had with students in Zaire that provoked insights that began to crystallize over the course of the eighth decade of my life.

I am in Kinshasa. The unrest here has reached a point where each night I must be brought to new, less endangered quarters. One time, I visited doctoral students in their rundown dormitories, where they live cramped into tiny spaces with their wives and children. The only table they have is a cooking surface, dining table, children's play area, and desk all-in-one, so that the expensive books and documents for their dissertations are constantly in danger. Despite unimaginable forbearance, these young men are nearing the goal of all their work. "What is the thing you most hope for in your future?" I ask them, thinking—admittedly—of riches and influence. The answer makes me speechless. "Once we have finished, we hope to resist the temptation to howl with the pack. We want to do it differently from those who have money and power. But continuing along that road is not easy; we must do without many things." Here is a radical new vision of the future. These pioneers' courage to swim against the stream goes to my heart and shatters my preconceived notions. It is revolutionary.

Over time, *revolution* becomes an important term for me. Admittedly, I use it half-jokingly, since it concerns something completely different from the revolutions we know from history. The revolution that this moment in world history demands of us must revolutionize even the accepted image of revolution. Until now, revolution has consisted of turning the respective power hierarchy on its head, so that the former revolutionaries climbed from the bottom to the top; otherwise everything remained the same. What is new is that the hierarchical power pyramid must be not only upturned but completely dismantled and replaced by a network. The Buddha made it his goal to put this into practice in his *sangha*,[1] and Jesus wanted to see it realized in his community of disciples: "The kings of the Gentiles lord it over them; and those in authority over them are called benefactors. But not so with you; rather the greatest among you must become like the youngest, and the leader like one who serves" (Luke 22:25–26). The doctoral students in Kinshasa obviously wanted something similar. Their clear vision and goal, like that of many other groups I was privileged to encounter, was not an improved power hierarchy but rather a network of mutual respect.

From the very beginning, the pyramid has been the fundamental model of our civilization, and most people have accepted and continue to accept that as a given. But—without a clear picture in their minds—they simultaneously desire something completely different. People blossom under mutual trust, but we wither under fear. Fear is the pyramidical method of power:

those at the top fear losing their power and, therefore, use violence to maintain their place. Further down in the pyramid, fear leads to rivalry and murderous competition. The fear of losing out leads to greed, jealousy, and envy. In a network, however, there is no position of power to defend, because all are equally worthy and thus equally empowered. Here, trust reigns instead of fear, cooperation instead of rivalry, communal sharing instead of greed.

History was never my favorite subject. Under Hitler, we were convinced that our history professors were lying to us, because all the past had to be tailored toward its glorious culmination in the Third Reich. But now I was tempted to examine the fundamental idea behind the French Revolution. Though the movement eventually turned completely in the wrong direction, I found its premise fascinating: "*Liberté, Égalité, Fraternité*"—did that not contain the program for the fresh start that was urgently needed even then but might today be necessary for our survival?

Freedom (*Liberté*) begins and ends with freedom from violence, to which I have sworn myself. Violence makes one unfree, since it is the perversion of power. The only creative use of power is the empowerment of others, and it frees the one who empowers no less than the one who knows himself empowered.

Equality (*Égalité*) does not mean razing everyone to the same level, but rather ensuring equality of rights. It became ever more clear to me that a dynamic order relies on this fundamental right. Where we conquer fear, competition turns into an interplay of give and take among people with equal rights—and equal duty.

Brotherliness (*Fraternité*) emphasizes equality by naming its origin: we all are part of the same human family. Simultaneously, it points to the most beautiful expression of familial encounter: sharing.

More than ever before, in my seventies I also had the opportunity of meeting people who stood at the helms of our society in the United States and elsewhere, and whom I could therefore presume to be well-informed. Again and again, I heard particularly the well-informed speak the words "We can't go on like this!"—not in politics, not in economics, and not in any other significant area either. "And why not?" I would ask. "Because we are in the process of destroying ourselves." (And, at that time, there were still many more who thoughtlessly exploited nature and the environment, calling climate change a hoax while still considering themselves experts.) Through violence, rivalry, and greed, we now stood at the brink of self-destruction. And in the thirty years since, we have come significantly closer. But during the same period, ever more people have woken up to the realization that our hope in the future lies in sharing, cooperation, and freedom from violence.

The pyramid hierarchy and the network proved to be helpful models for understanding my own personal experience in this period of my life. At its beginning (1994–97), I was teacher-in-residence at the Esalen Institute on the California coast at Big Sur, close to the New Camaldoli Hermitage with which I was closely connected, as I related earlier. Archaeological finds have shown that even five thousand years ago, Native Americans of the Esselen tribe and their ancestors had their winter grounds near the hot springs at this place that nature endowed so richly. In our time, more and more young people have settled here, living in the style of the counterculture of the early 1960s and questioning the prevalent social order. The spark that kindled Esalen's future was the idea to invite intellectual pioneers of the time as teachers and guides: Abraham Maslow, Joan Baez, Paul Tillich, Henry Miller, Fritz Perls, Timothy Leary, Carl Rogers—even a cursory and incomplete listing is impressive. Hot springs by a steep cliff face above the thundering bay; bathing pools overlooking the sea and the playgrounds of whales, dolphins, and sea otters: all that was seductive enough to attract even the most prominent of guests without a speaking fee. Soon, the retreat developed into a non-profit center for humanistically oriented interdisciplinary studies and conventions. The center was owned by the community and run professionally as a business.

Perhaps equally important was the fact that the massage technique that developed there soon grew in fame, and that gardeners coaxed not only indescribably glorious flowers from the fertile soil but also rich harvests of fresh vegetables, which inventive chefs turned into delicious vegetarian meals. Several of the women began a kindergarten to care for the children of families employed there, and soon guests too discovered that their little ones were well cared for at the progressively run *Gazebo* and enjoyed playing with the goats, dogs, and donkeys. Meanwhile, parents were free to participate in the courses or enjoy the hot springs. The various talents of the community found rich expression and use, and the venture thrived.

Mike Murphy and Dick Price, both born in 1930, had been colleagues at Stanford University and, in 1961, founded the Esalen Institute together. Mike inherited most of the land (where the young people of the Beat generation had settled) from his family: his grandfather, a doctor, had already considered making therapeutic use of the hot springs before there were roads leading to Esalen. As a disciple of Sri Aurobindo, Mike meditated with conviction and tenacity, but soon focused more on his writing and felt particularly responsible for the commercial unfolding of Esalen, which he furthered with the help of a supervisory board. Soon, he moved to San Francisco, many hours away by car. Dick, by contrast, continued to live in the community and was connected to it by mutual love and appreciation. Together with his wife, Chris, he was role model, inspiration, and communal center to the varied crowd who were doing pioneering work here. He had had bad personal experiences with psychiatric practices, and wanted to make Esalen a place of psychological healing, where inner processes could unfold organically and find balance. Using the therapeutic method that he developed, he was successful, and he gave Esalen the orientation that would make it a world-famous center of integral healing for body and soul.

On November 25, 1985, Dick was—as he did so often—meditating high in the hills near the spring supplying Esalen with water when he was hit by a falling rock and killed. (At the very same time, something moved me out of the blue to hold a speech of praise in his honor, even though I was over three thousand miles away and knew nothing of his death.) The passing of this man who had decisively shaped Esalen's inner life for more than twenty years was a blow that would forever change the direction of his and Mike Murphy's creation. Although Steve Donovan, the new director, was trusted by both the community and the supervisory board and did everything in his power to bridge the gap, the goals of the board and the community drifted further and further apart. Steve began to invite "teachers-in-residence": women and men who might support the unsure community by their presence and charisma. I was one of those honored with an invitation. In one of those almost too dramatic moments of fate, the moment I arrived and put my suitcase down, Steve embraced me and left Esalen for good.

There I now stood, in between the "village community"—as I viewed those who had come to Esalen in the early days with their families—and the "entrepreneurs," who saw it as their responsibility to turn Esalen into a profitable venture. On the one hand, women and men who had often worked and lived here for half their life and had raised children here claimed a kind of authorial right: had they not made Esalen what it was? Did the guests not come because of the warm atmosphere of community that they had created and which could not live on in that way without them? On the other hand, the board considered that it had not only the right but the duty to transform the confusing welter of community into a well-organized staff. To this day, I do not know whether that was even truly in the realm of possibility at the time. With more experience and empathy, the tensions might have been eased and the sudden, unexplained dismissals of honored longtime colleagues might have been avoided. But beyond that, it was a question of principle.

In retrospect, it seems that this was a small-scale demonstration of the contrast between network and pyramid hierarchy. While Esalen has done considerable service in programs for businesspeople—I myself was privileged to participate in several conferences at which entrepreneurs and groundbreaking pioneers in the field of economics introduced new, more humane models of leadership—Esalen still followed the conventional administrative model, and the hopes of Dick Price and the community's original network belonged to the past.

The time at Esalen was very difficult, and my heart still grows heavy when I recall the suffering I witnessed. But I remain deeply thankful for the encounters and experiences that were given to me there. After my years in California, I once again returned to New York and now felt that I had reached the end of my life. At that time, my friends Nancy and Roderich Graeff settled down in a Quaker retirement home not far from our monastery and offered the option of housing me there as well. Father Martin, familiar with the difficulties of caring for aging brothers, gratefully accepted the offer on my behalf. And thus, Kendal at Ithaca became a new kind of hermitage for me that turned out to be exactly what I needed. I did not travel anymore, reduced all contact to a minimum, and prepared to die. Well, life was to unfold differently. Again, and again, friends had urged me to put texts on the internet. I was not overly interested, but Daniel Uvanovic, an adventurous young internet expert whom I had gotten to know in Big Sur when he went to the monastery for a retreat, offered to visit me in Ithaca for several weeks and build a website for me. We selected gratitude as a theme. The weeks turned into years, and the humble beginnings turned into a source of strength for the worldwide network of tens of thousands of visitors daily. (In my heart, I gratefully carry the names—far too many to list them all here—of the many friends and colleagues who made it possible.) The Fetzer Institute, a foundation that gave us a starting grant, asked two questions to which we were supposed to find the answers: (1) Is the internet suited to spirituality? And (2) can one build a community on the internet?

Today, the answers have become so obvious that they sound like trick questions: the internet has enabled countless new forms of community. In and of itself, it can be understood as a frame for the network that Pierre Teilhard de Chardin called the *noösphere*—essentially a network of all-connecting love that spans and unites the world. The further-reaching and more intensive this network, the more encompassing and deep is its aliveness. Life is connection, and if spirituality is liveliness by its very name (the Latin *spiritus* means "breath of life"), then the cyber network is itself a spiritual phenomenon, since it leads to increased aliveness through connection.

The closer our website comes to its goal, the more revolutionary—and contemplative—it will be.[2] Our goal is to connect people the world over, all of whom support one another in living a grateful and joyful life. However, anything aiming for a networked connection in our society dictated by pyramid hierarchies of power is revolutionary. And the things that seek to be revolutionary in the true sense must be contemplative.

It is a widespread misconception that *contemplative* must mean "turned away from the world." As early as my novitiate, I learned from Father Damasus how important the little syllable *con-* is for understanding contemplative life. Just like the Latin *cum* ("with"), it indicates connection. The things that are to be connected in contemplation are an ideal image and its realization. Looking up at the sky shows us an eternal order, represented by the constellations, and this presentation is realized amid the world's chaos by the building of a temple. The syllable *temp* is ancient and originally means "measure." By looking up at the heavens, a contemplative person gains the measure by which the temple will be built, which is why the earliest temples—such as Stonehenge—are something like giant sundials or star clocks. And in India, there is a saying: "When the temple's measurements are right, there is order in the world." As human beings, we are called to look up at the sky even by our upright gait, and our free hands permit us to turn the ideal image into tangible reality: "on earth as it is in heaven."

In this way, my work with others on the website becomes a new form of living contemplatively and sharing this life with untold numbers of people. At the same time, this turns out to be the beginning of that revolution to which I have felt duty bound. To my astonishment, my life continues. A whole new period of my life opens before me.

DIALOGUE

JK: At first glance, mysticism and politics do not seem to fit together too well. We think of mysticism as a kind of interiority that is highly personal and thus not comprehensible or accessible to others. And politics, too, is often simplified to the public exercise of power and its strategic preservation. You consider mysticism and politics together in your word pair of *contemplation* and *revolution*. Why is this impulse for social change so important to spirituality?

DSR: Understood correctly, spirituality means aliveness. The term comes from *spiritus*, the life breath. Full aliveness means being awake to the responsibility we have in the face of the Great Mystery, but also to the responsibility we have in the face of the community, the *polis*—politics. In this field, too, spirituality is an awakening. If we sleep through our responsibility to the public good, we are not as spiritual as we should be. Not fully awake; not fully alive.

JK: As far back as Greek antiquity there was a distinction between the *polites*, those who were interested in and working toward the public good, and the *idiotes*, those who thought for themselves in private and were active only for their own prospects.

DSR: So, we do not want to be idiots.

JK: Regarding the revolutionary: In which spiritual tradition do you see yourself there? What role models are you thinking of?

DSR: Above all others, my role model is Jesus Christ as a revolutionary. He was one in his time and was recognized as such. Death by crucifixion was not a punishment for religious transgressions; those were punished by stoning. Crucifixion was an overtly political punishment, reserved for escaped slaves and revolutionaries—for transgressions by which the so-called criminal had undermined the existing social order. Jesus did that by preaching about the coming kingdom of God. When he says, "The greatest among you will be your servant," he is undermining the power pyramid of the time—and of our time as well. Is that not decidedly revolutionary?

JK: What did he radically question at the time that we might still profit from today?

DSR: The abuse of power. In our surroundings, we all have more power than we think: over children, friends, acquaintances, colleagues, family, and so on. The only legitimate use of this power consists in empowering others. If we do not do this, then power turns to violence. Violence seeks to control, subjugate, exploit. That was the primary thing Jesus turned against.

JK: Empower others, yes, but empower to what end?

DSR: Empower them to actualize themselves living in community, to bring forth their best creatively.

JK: Living their full potential.

DSR: Precisely. What parents do for their children and teachers do for their students, if they are doing it right: getting the best out of them.

JK: Can that also work in conditions of scarcity and crisis?

DSR: Crisis? Scarcity? The idea of scarcity is an interpretation arising from a lack of trust in life. We cannot allow ourselves this mistaken interpretation of the situation. If we live out of a consciousness of abundance, which is much more realistic than the idea of scarcity, we will also approach crises completely differently. Then the crisis is no longer the end of everything.

JK: And no longer without alternatives.

DSR: Absolutely! The word *crisis* comes from the same root word as *sieve*. *Crisis* means "winnowing out." In every crisis, all that is capable of life becomes separated from what is no longer capable of survival. There is a similar process in nature: when it pulls off the dried husks so that the young shoots can unfold freely.

JK: But one can also misinterpret that as Social Darwinism or misuse it for certain economic interpretations, such as, only those best adapted to the system survive—survival of the fittest. The strong then have the advantage over the weak because the latter have not had as much opportunity, are less well-educated, or had the misfortune of being born in the wrong time, in the wrong place. Then fate, as it were, spits the weak onto the rubbish heap of history.

DSR: I do not want to deny that. But I would say yes, the strongest survive, and what is strongest is not violence but cooperation. Working together with others makes us stronger, that is, cooperation in service of the common good. Building one another up rather than keeping one another down. That is what I mean. The strongest are those who recognize that what makes us strong is that we orient ourselves in the direction of life, and life aims at cooperation, connection, networks.

JK: Coevolution?

DSR: Yes, coevolution. The strongest are those who recognize that and contribute to coevolution. That is how it has always been. We can read this fundamental rule in the past.

JK: In what do you read that, for example?

DSR: In the development of life—otherwise I do not think it would have evolved this far. It is a misinterpretation to think that competition was the only force moving evolution forward. In that approach, we are forgetting about motherly love, for example. The supposedly strong would never have grown up if, at all stages of evolution, there had not been the strong mother caring for her weak children. We forget that too easily.

JK: We also forget fatherly love.

DSR: It may be autobiographically typical that I am forgetting to mention that.

JK: It has its qualities too, of course.
    To return to your role models. You have already mentioned Jesus. Are there any contemporary role models as well?

DSR: Yes. I can immediately think of a woman I have admired and venerated: Dorothy Day, who founded the Catholic Worker Movement.[3]

JK: That is an organization that dedicates itself to those cast out by society.

DSR: Yes, and this organization is still extraordinarily alive and successful. It grew out of Dorothy's compassion for the poor and her insight that poverty in the United States cannot go on like this, and then other communities grew out of her initial founding with Peter Maurin in 1933 in New York. Just like Mother Teresa, she cared for the poorest of the poor, but she went beyond that and questioned the social structure responsible for such poverty. That is why she was repeatedly imprisoned. Brazilian archbishop Hélder Câmara understood that when he said, "If I give food to the poor, I am called a Holy Man; if I ask why the poor are poor, I am called a Communist." Several Christian communities in Latin America also questioned the pyramid hierarchies of power based on their reading of the glad tidings of Jesus. Such approaches are often denounced as Communist.

JK: Correctly or incorrectly?

DSR: Correctly in the best sense of communist, meaning reflecting community, but incorrectly in the sense of the political Communist International movement.

JK: So, the Communist party ideology.

DSR: Precisely.

JK: In your pair of terms—*contemplation* and *revolution*—you redefined revolution as the end of the hierarchical power pyramid and the rise of communities organized as networks. At first glance, that seems admirable, and I think I understand the kind of networks you have in mind. But to clarify, I will offer a critical counterargument, and as a devil's advocate, consciously misinterpret you. A subversive nongovernmental organization like the Mafia has recently also begun to organize as a network. Even terrorist organizations like the so-called Islamic State, with its streamlined, autonomously acting cells and network structures, have been highly successful in their attacks in Belgium, France, and Turkey. If a network has inward trust, that does not necessarily say anything about the ethics of that networked organization, only about its effectiveness. So, I am afraid that the new spirit you have in mind cannot be attributed solely to the form of organization.

DSR: No, not to the form of organization but to its use of power. The question is whether power is used to empower everyone in their independence. That is important. It must count for everyone. It must encompass all human beings, not merely a specific group.

JK: Meaning, the networks you are picturing have a universalist orientation?

DSR: Universalist and borne by respect for every individual person. But *respect* may be too pale a term. It is about deep care toward your neighbor, toward all other people, and toward life in all its forms. This great care, this reverence for life must be central.

JK: So, what Albert Schweitzer said: "I am life that wants to live, in the middle of life that wants to live."

DSR: Precisely that. That would be the spirituality of the networks I am referring to, and that fundamentally distinguishes them from those of the Mafia and the terrorists.

JK: You describe how in the 1990s, as a teacher at the legendary Esalen Institute in Big Sur, you had the opportunity of seeing these differing organizational structures—the pyramid and the network—firsthand, including their consequences. The community that had grown in and around Esalen wanted to live precisely this innovative, supportive, empowering network. In the end, however, a traditional model prevailed, with a board controlling the business. Is it possible that all-too-human motives worked more strongly there than an altruistic, cooperative spirit? Might these networks you are describing not also require, in the widest sense, a reformed human, or conditions for human cohabitation that are not a given in our social system?

DSR: I believe that we need a new consciousness to fully realize the necessary change. The pressure of the old, the power of the old is very great. It takes great effort and courage to resist this pressure. And in Esalen, unfortunately, that did not succeed.

JK: Why?

DSR: It simply does not always work. Courage and strength are not always enough.

JK: It probably also takes patience—it takes a long time to drill through thick boards—to stand the pressure that one might be exposed to for a long time.

DSR: Again and again I ask myself, Has everything there really been simply destroyed? We look back and see that over the course of our history, there have always been little groups—demonized in our history books, because history is written by the powerful— that have attempted to realize the ideal of setting the power of love against the love of power. These attempts have always been foiled in some way. For example, I am thinking of farmers' riots, which certainly went in this direction often.

JK: One can see the same thing when one looks at religious orders such as the Franciscans, who were quite revolutionary in the beginning. They were only able to survive because there was a humble pope.

DSR: In their original form, the Franciscans did not survive; they became something else in their second generation. The Rule of their order was changed, and even the original stories were altered and censored. That makes me wonder was that simply the end of it all? Personally, the only answer I can find to that question is Hölderlin's verse:

Life's lines, like mountain's boundary
Or paths, change, vary, and differ.
To what we are here, a God may there confer
Peace, eternal grace, and harmony.[4]

I believe that all positive efforts will be completed from beyond time. I cannot give any evidence of this, but the good, the true, the beautiful is lasting and, to a certain degree, is not subject to time. All self-sacrifice that we dedicate to the true, the beautiful, and the good, and especially the effort we expend for it, cannot be lost. I cannot say any more. We need this conviction or else we would despair.

JK: The dominant model of thought propagated so successfully in the 1990s and still prevalent today is the idea of competition: we all are competing with one another, and that has been implemented even in the educational system. Advocates of this model argue that the competitive idea is ingrained in human nature, the goal is merely to steer it toward the good of society. One can see it in kindergarten where children compete for the best toys and the teacher's affection; then in school, they compete for the best grades; at work, we compete for the best position, or the biggest paycheck; in art and culture, we compete for the highest degree of recognition; politicians compete for votes. Wherever we look, there is competition. But competition also means that there are winners and losers. Deep within us, we have learned that without competition, there would be no drive to expend effort and develop ourselves, to do something great. Therefore, it seems that competition and selection are important drivers of progress. Is that true, in your opinion?

DSR: Only to a degree. The idea of competition as we know it contains two aspects: the desire to surpass, and the desire to outdo someone else. Those two things are different, and simply so intertwined in our thinking that we can hardly tell the difference. But the difference is there.

JK: The difference might be between being good and being better than someone else.

DSR: Wanting to be good, wanting to surpass oneself is positive. But measuring how good I am based on how far down I can push someone else is wrong because it is destructive of life. We can see that in nature as well. Here, every plant wants to realize itself and its inward life, not suppress the others.

JK: There are also weeds that will outgrow other plants and spread at the cost of the others.

DSR: That is interpretation. Not at the cost of others. They want to spread and do, but not in any fight against the other plants. Seeing that as a fight is an interpretation that we put on what we observe. The other plant must simply unfold even more in its way, and that may mean that it needs to change. That is mutual influence.

JK: But in the plant world, there is also displacement. For example, several years ago, a plant from the Himalayas was introduced to the Alps and is crowding out endemic species on a massive scale simply because it is so much heartier. So, the image may not quite work.

DSR: But that crowding out is a byproduct of self-expression, not its goal, that is the difference. For us as human beings, the highest goal is self-expression and the cooperation of all. I remember a report about American Indian children who were given a soccer ball. They played with it enthusiastically, but as soon as they were divided into groups and had to play against one another, they completely lost interest. Their joy came from the play *with* each other, not *against* each other.

JK: I find that playing against each other has its charm as well, so long as it is a game and does not create shame or fear.

DSR: And so long as one can feel joy if the other wins.

JK: I play soccer with others, and I also want to shoot a goal myself. But when someone else from my team has that opportunity, I am overjoyed with him.

DSR: Can I not also feel joy when the other team scores a goal? Is it about winning against the opposite team, or is it about an enthusiastic joint game? The better I play, the better I encourage others to play. That is competition as it is supposed to be, not as it is.

JK: Competition in quality, not competition for resources.

DSR: Yes, those are helpful concepts in this very difficult area. One aspect of competition, the highest possible degree of self-actualization, drives development and progress and should be viewed positively.

JK: The other idea of competition divides people into the successful—the winners—and the losers. We see that in the world at large: some economies are designed to leave others behind, and that has social consequences when competition leaves those other nations behind in their race for social and economic development. From the point of view of the system, that cannot be healthy.

DSR: The system is the important thing. One must look at the larger picture and see how the success of the individual affects that. In the larger framework, surpassing oneself should be seen positively, but to me, self-actualization at the cost of others does not seem to support the system at large.

JK: Primarily because it comes from a wrong experience of the self. In the end, we are always from others, through others, and toward others.

DSR: True. This view of things does come from an isolated, cut-off, outcast, and thus "sinful" I, from the Ego and not from the I-Self that knows itself connected with all others.

JK: Ever since Descartes, this Ego has additionally been living in a bubble, imagining that it is only an I because it thinks. But thinking is only one possible self-description of a human being. By contrast, one might also say, he is, because he feels compassion, or is connected, or because he is at all—from the point of view of existence.

I was surprised that in the French Revolution's apparently secular program of *Liberté, Fraternité, Égalité* you see a program for new social order. You know that after the Revolution, thousands went to the guillotine in the name of these ideals. After the revolutionary impulse of liberation, a state terrorist regime followed, which was finally ended by another nationalist leader, in this case Napoleon, who tried to extend an imperialist reign over all of Europe. Why do you believe that with liberty, equality, and brotherliness, we might have found a program for a new social order on which our lives may even depend?

DSR: Yes, of course the French Revolution ended up completely antithetical to its origins. But the original idea of liberty, equality, and brotherliness is—forgetting for a moment that erroneous development and looking only at the concepts themselves—the exact thing that Jesus Christ tried to realize. The greatest among you shall not rule over the others but serve them. You are all brothers.

JK: So, you would see love for your neighbor as a brotherly love?

DSR: Yes, because we are all children of God.

JK: Today, liberty is enthusiastically advocated in the West but also elsewhere in the world. We want to be free and understand this freedom as very individual. But what we do not see enough is that there are societies that are captive; that is, that we also need liberation within society, not liberation of the individual for his or her own autonomous choices. The freedom of choice in our Western societies is very great. But liberty is also connected with justice and equality. We like to overlook that. I am thinking of a global justice, seeing the world as a system.

DSR: Justice is the order that comes from rights and duties. What we call justice today is the same thing of which the Romans said, "*Summum ius summa iniuria*" (extreme justice is extreme injustice). Justice as we see it in the criminal justice system, for example, is merely legalized revenge, as far as I am concerned. I was very pleased that, regarding criminal justice, the Argentinian constitution states (I am paraphrasing), "Crime should not be punished but corrected and prevented in the future." True justice belongs in a context of restitution and healing, not of revenge and punishment. In the case of a crime, that means—without excusing or minimizing it—helping the criminal to become a solid member of society again instead of simply punishing or executing him.

JK: In Europe, we are currently experiencing the end of the economic growth model as we knew it even into the end of the 1990s. Our economies are no longer growing, or growing only insignificantly. At the same time, industrialized countries can no longer afford the road of expansive growth, purely for ecological reasons. If we want to realize the climate goals of limiting global warming to 1.5°C as set down by the United Nations in the 2015 Paris Agreement, that means that we need to quickly stop using fossil fuels and at least halve our use of resources, which would lead to a radical change in the Western lifestyle. If we do not manage that, we risk catastrophic climate events that will endanger our lives. We will see even greater wars and refugee movements than we do today, which is something we wish neither for ourselves nor our children. Pope Francis has recognized and stated this clearly in his encyclical *Laudato si'*. Where do you see the duty of religion in these linked political, ecological, and economic questions? Does it have a duty there?

DSR: Yes, if we understand the word *religion* to also mean a reconnection of broken bonds: bonds between us and our true selves; between us and all others; between us and the Great Mystery, then the correction of our ecologically destructive activity is unquestionably a part of it. Pope Francis understood it correctly. As almost the only one in this sphere, he keeps pointing clearly to the connection between the destruction of the environment and the social destruction that is its consequence. That is revolutionary and arises from his deeply contemplative insight.

JK: In this context, he used strong words: "Such an economy kills."[5]

DSR: Yes! It is high time that religious representatives speak out in this regard.

JK: Not only speak out, but also live as role models within their institutions. I was astonished that already in your early 70s, you were preparing for your eventual death. Not that it is completely unrealistic to engage with the idea of death, because we move toward death from our birth. But it surprised me how rationally you dealt with it. You moved to an old person's home in Ithaca,

I Am Because of You

New York, which had been recommended to you by good friends. But it evidently all turned out very differently. What made that possible?

DSR: The thing that pulled me back from this kind of retreat was the creation of the website "Grateful Living," which, initially, I did not regard as a task pointing me to the future. My friends recommended it and insisted on the need for a website. So, we made this website,[6] which became a kind of seed that suddenly burst forth.

JK: You mean that it fell on such fertile ground that it now has versions all over the world?

DSR: That was unforeseeable. But after I had some coresponsibility for this website and wanted to do justice to that responsibility, I was called back out of my reclusiveness to contribute, and that includes my travels now. So, one thing led to another.

JK: This "Grateful Living" network—what is it, and what isn't it? Could you go into more detail about the fundamental reason behind it? What makes it so attractive and a possible alternative for people from completely different cultures and religious backgrounds?

DSR: The power of this idea illustrates that gratitude speaks to all people, that there is no person who does not see gratitude as a positive value. So, gratitude connects people, and we are in urgent need of that today. All religions emphasize that gratitude is an important value. In it we have a value that is easily understandable for any child and is universally recognized. That is why today there seems to be a wave of gratitude spreading throughout the world, which is what we wanted to achieve with the website. From the very beginning, it was conceived as a tool, as support for offline groups making an effort to live gratefully—small groups of gratitude all over the world, small networks that connect with one another. This idea has proved itself. Of course, we quickly arrived at these questions: For what are we truly thankful? Can we be thankful for everything? And that led us to our next task for the site: to explain the concept of gratitude.

JK: How would you explain what gratitude is about and what it is not about?

DSR: Grateful living is an attempt to face life and its challenges with gratitude in each moment.

JK: And why with gratitude?

DSR: Because the present moment, with all the possibilities it offers, is the greatest gift one can imagine. In everything there is a gift to everything else there is. When we recognize that and live by it, we connect with all living things in each moment. That goes far beyond anything one imagines in that first instant when one thinks of gratitude. Unpacking, thinking through, and then spreading that concept is the goal of this website.

JK: Let me play devil's advocate once again, because I can imagine people who say, "Brother David is calling me to gratitude. So now I need to be grateful to be a good person. It's suddenly my new duty and in a way an effort. But if I look at my life, there are all these blows of fate, so many things for which I am not grateful. I'm lucky to have survived all the illness and death around me. Thank heavens I'm still alive!"

DSR: The most important keyword for grateful life is *opportunity*.
Even the most hideous situations keep giving us opportunities for being grateful. Blows of fate and difficulties often give us completely new opportunities for proving ourselves, for learning, for growth, and maybe even for creative protest. Those might often be gifts we did not wish for, but by living with a grateful attitude, we can use the opportunities that we have received.

177

A grateful life is a creative life because we learn to ask of each moment, What is this opportunity for? If we use the opportunity, we show ourselves to be creative. Grateful living means creative living. The alternative would be simply to fold in on ourselves and say, "Life got to me." But even in that we have an opportunity that we might have never chosen but that can yield entirely new things.

JK: Even the fight for more justice in social conflicts—that too is a form of grateful living.

DSR: Definitely. This insight—with which I am in complete agreement—points to the fact that we often think far too individually about grateful living. Life is always about connection. It is not simply about individual acts of gratitude but about grateful living. Life means connection—in the end, unbounded connection. That is why social responsibility is always a part of grateful life.

JK: That sounds a little like a strategy for happiness.

DSR: Yes, the longing for happiness drives a grateful life. As people, what we are looking for in the end is lasting happiness—happiness that does not depend on whether we succeed at any specific thing. We call this type of happiness "joy," and joy even in unhappiness is a real possibility for people. There is a saying that "happiness is round," meaning it does not come to rest anywhere but rolls away and passes. But joy, which in the end does come only from gratitude, is something we can always preserve, even in times of unhappiness.

JK: That means that I do not need to be happy first in order to be grateful.

DSR: On the contrary, I need to be grateful first, and that will make me happy.

JK: Why is that the case?

DSR: Because joy is identical to gratitude. If we give children something and they get joy from it, we know that they are grateful, even if they do not say "thank you." If they say "thank you," then they are also well-socialized and well brought up. But true gratitude is joy. That is true of gratitude in general, even with adults. Living with joy means living gratefully, and living with gratitude means living joyfully.

Peace demonstration with Zentatsu Richard Baker Roshi (center) and Thich Nhat Hanh (center-right); New York, June 12, 1982

9

DOUBLE REALM

2006–2016

As a young man on one of my first visits to New York City, I walked up Fifth Avenue one evening and, at 59th Street, wandered into the southeast corner of Central Park and into a small zoo. Most of the zoo's regular visitors were children, and at this late hour, I was there alone. But suddenly, I felt a powerful presence, looked up, and saw a gorilla sitting on the roof of his house. His massive form seemed to tower hugely in the dusk, and yet he was sitting there hunched over, as if grieving. As I approached, I could see into his eyes, but it seemed that he hardly noticed me, as if his thoughts were somewhere far away. He was old, maybe very old. I cannot say how long we stayed like that, holding each other's gaze, but I know that it was a long time. Long enough to tell me something about aging, a suspicion deep enough that I still have not fully plumbed it, not even in the last decade of my life so far—I say "so far" because I have learned to expect surprises, and because there do remain mysteries that wait to be explored.

In this stage of my life, the plumb bob of my contemplation will keep returning to depths for which I find helpful a key word of Rilke. Often, the poet speaks of the "double realm":

181

I Am Because of You

And though the pool's reflection
often blurs before us:
Know the image.

Only in the double realm
do the voices become
eternal and mild.[1]

This image can be used in many situations, and it is important to remember that the double realm is an inseparable unit, though my thinking keeps wanting to pull its two aspects apart. Distinguish—yes! Separate—no. Looking at the whole, with as all-encompassing an eye as possible, without permitting it to fall apart in my imagination: I see that as my great task in aging.

T. S. Eliot points out this difficulty:

Let me disclose the gifts reserved for age
To set a crown upon your lifetime's effort...
As body and soul begin to fall asunder.[2]

On some days, it really does seem as though everything were about to fall asunder: my spelt roll falls out of my hands into the full plate of soup and splatters my white robe with pumpkin soup and seed oil from head to toe—black and yellow in the Emperor's colors. Is this my "second childhood"? During my first childhood, I know that my mother told me, while laughing, that the first time I saw a plate of spinach soup in front of me on the table, I was so excited about the green that I put both hands into the bowl and smeared it on myself from top to bottom. Now, too, the brothers laugh kindly at my little accident in the refectory and suggest, "Perhaps one could call it 'art in action'!" That is at least a more positive interpretation than that all is falling asunder.

But why does it seem so natural to talk of the body and soul falling apart in aging and death? Because I am aware that, on the one hand, my soul, my self, lives in the Now and is thus not bound by time, while my body, on the other hand, has a beginning and is moving toward my daily approaching end. So, in my body, I am tied to time, and my I is ephemeral, while my self has permanence. And yet I experience myself as a unit, as *I myself*—not as *I* and *self*. However, I am aware of this unity only so long as I live in the Now, in the moment, in the double realm of time and eternity. As soon as I hold on to the past or become entangled in fantasies of the future, I am aware only of the passage of time and the fact that my time is slipping away. ("I'm slipping, I'm slipping away, like sand slipping through fingers," says the poet.)[3] More than ever, I consider it the great task of my life to keep returning to the Now and to recognize that the time and eternity I move between do not lie next to each other but rather entwined in one another. I am living in the dynamic tension of the *one* double realm.

On my travels, I have no difficulty with this. I must simply live in the Now. And in my old age, I am frequently given the gift of travel—more often, more distant, and more thrilling than ever before. That is due in part to the fact that I can no longer travel alone. I can no longer hear the announcements in airports clearly; I need glasses to read the signs, and often those glasses are hidden away in my luggage; and a younger generation is simply more adept and reliable at scanning electronic boarding passes. So, I kept my eyes open for a younger traveling companion, and I found Anthony Chavez, who had just finished his college degree and wanted to help me. As an old man, it was a new experience for me to show this young man far-off countries. While it was possibly even more fun for me than for him, we both enjoyed it. In the late autumn of my life, it was also a joy to see this young man blossom, and I was as proud as a grandfather when he worked for and found his dream job in education.

Without a companion, my travels now took on a new form, but they did not become fewer and they did not become shorter.

I Am Because of You

On the contrary: I was to get to know a whole continent completely new to me—South America. New friends, Alberto and Lizzie Rizzo from Buenos Aires, were enthusiastic about gratitude and worked with amazing assiduity at sharing the joy of grateful living with thousands, just as my friends Peter Kessler, Brigitte Kwizda-Gredler, and Mirjam Luthe-Alves had begun to do in Europe. To my great joy, websites, workshops, seminars, and practice groups developed on both continents, through the enthusiasm, devotion, and effort of volunteers. In Argentina, I felt received and surrounded by such a warm outpouring of maternal energy that I now revere the maternal side of the Great Mystery—which I had already encountered in the Mariazeller Mother of God as a child, and later found in the Virgin of Guadalupe—in the image of Nuestra Señora de Luján. I entrust myself to her protection when flying back to Argentina, whether to shoot a film in Patagonia, engage in a dialogue with Father Anselm Grün before a thousand readers at the Buenos Aires book fair, or simply to enjoy the overwhelming waterfalls of Iguazú. Yes, in my old age, friends gift me even with such "pleasure trips." In this new phase of my travels, I let myself be placed on a direct flight and be picked up at the airport. That way, I can still manage it.

At the same time, I keep making journeys inward to new regions of the double realm. It is undivided and indivisibly one, and my journeys into its depths are not a departure from what seems a surface. No, eternity appears *in* time and space—shines out, throws light on my path. All that lies behind me on this path was necessary to bring me to this precise place, and everything before me can be reached only from this current vantage point. Rilke helps me name what lies before me, waiting to be discovered: "inner world-space," "the open," the "middle inside," "the nameless," finally "the inaccessible"—the Mystery. It is big and simple. The things that I become aware of looking back, by contrast, are multitudinous in their thousands of networked connections.

Much more often than before, I think about my ancestors,

try to imagine them, far back. My right palm exhibits Dupuytren's contracture, which does not bother me, but reminds me that I might have inherited it from Viking ancestors.[4] What raids might lie in my past, or what pogroms, in which my noble Polish ancestors might have massacred my Hasidic Jewish forebears. How did these strands flow together into one person? The word *person* comes from Roman vocabulary and used to mean "the role, the mask through which an actor's voice sounded" (*per* means "through," and *sonare* means "to sound"). What coincidences might have led me to play the role I play today? Yes, I can imagine the relationship between my "I" in the river of time and my "Self" beyond time well in the metaphor of role-playing. The entire unpredictable past defined the role that is now given to me. So much was determined at my birth—my sex, my skin color, the family and culture I was born into, thousands of other unchangeable givens.

On the first Sunday of each month, the brothers in the Gut Aich monastery put on a puppet show after the children's service. One and the same brother can play two characters: the sidekick, Seppl, with one hand, for example, and the crocodile with the other. In the same way, the one grand Self can play countless roles as well. My Self, which is at home in the Great Self, thus plays the role assigned to me. In playing, Self and I become one; I can distinguish between them but never separate them.

I ask myself what it means to play my role "well." The answer must be: Playing the role well means playing with love—expressing a yes to boundless mutual belonging. If the I denies this yes, the Self nevertheless gives it the strength to play on, but the I is playing its role "poorly."

"But everything is only beautiful out of love! But everything is only good out of love!"[5] But what if the Self—to retain the metaphor—takes off the hand puppet, or the mask decays into dust? Is everything over, everything at an end? I would say that it is indeed at an end, but it is not over. I do not want to speak of a "life *after* death." If dying means that my time is at an end, then it makes no sense to speak of something "after." But even now everything I experience has a dimension that transcends time and space. T. S. Eliot calls the Now "the moment in and out of time"—it belongs in time and yet not.[6] In the double realm of the Now, time and eternity are one, so I cannot ever lose even the smallest detail of all that I hold dear here. "All is always now," says T. S. Eliot—speaking a truth that cannot be denied, because what is not now is not, and has only a shadow reality in past or future. But in the Now it cannot be lost: it is no longer in effect, like a law might pass out of effect, it has been lifted, as to a higher level, and it is kept like a gold bracelet is kept safe and treasured in a vault. In this sense, I understand why Rilke sees our life goal in storing up our experiences: "We are the bees of the universe, passionately securing the nectar of the visible and storing it in the great golden honeycomb of the invisible."[7]

Can I then even feel anxious about dying? Yes, I do feel anxiety. I admit it, but I do not want to be afraid. Anxiety and fear are two things. The word *anxiety* takes its root from a word meaning "tightness and narrowness" and that is certainly not a coincidence. As human beings, our primeval experience of anxiety is the narrowness of the birth canal. We go through this first bottleneck with instinctive trust; we must later learn to engage with all anxiety as fearlessly and spontaneously as we did at birth. Fear and trust are two attitudes that are diametrically opposed. In the end, both are attitudes, because, while anxiety is unavoidable in life, we can choose between fear and courage. Fear resists anxiety and thus becomes stuck; courage engages anxiety with trust and thus finds a way out. In that moment, courage does not take away the anxiety. In fact, the obverse is the case: without anxiety, there is no need for courage. But if we trust in anxiety throughout life, then life itself will lead us through our anxieties to a new birth. I prove that to myself. I look back at the bottlenecks of my life—the moments when my life narrowed—and see quite clearly: the more pressing the anxiety, the more brilliant the surprising new things that resulted from it. Reminding myself of that again and again gives me trust in life and the courage to die.

What also helps me is the role model of people whose death I have witnessed. Here, I recall two brothers from Mount Saviour: The first is Brother Christopher who oversaw the work of building the monastery. Though he was only forty, he had severe heart problems, and on this day, he was the reader before lunch. As server, I stood next to him when he began the reading: "But that same night the word of the LORD came to Nathan: Go and tell my servant David: Thus says the LORD: Are you the one to build me a house to live in?" Six verses later, he came to this place in the reading: "Moreover the LORD declares to you that the LORD will make you a house" (2 Sam 7:4–5, 11). Then he quietly laid his head on the book and was dead. The second person is our Father James Kelly (we had to use his last name, as we had two brothers named James) who went into the chapel one last time on the evening of Holy Saturday and whispered with the enthusiasm that was so typical of him: "I cannot wait for tomorrow!" Then he went to bed. In the morning, he was supposed to sing the *Exsultet*, but it seems that he really could not wait and was now singing it in heaven.

About a week before my mother's death—she is already quite weak—Vanja Palmers, whom she loves like a son, comes to visit her from Switzerland. He tells her that today, on St. Martin's Day, there is a tradition in Sursee in Switzerland that children can earn pieces of cheese for pulling the most outrageous face. Though we do not set out cheese as our prize, we nevertheless all try to make more outrageous faces than the others. My mother, on her death bed, outdoes us all.

In his famous poem "Sailing to Byzantium," William Butler Yeats compares an old man to a decrepit scarecrow:

> ...unless
> Soul clap its hands and sing, and louder sing
> For every tatter in its mortal dress."[8]

I try to do that whenever something about my "mortal dress" has once again gone to tatters, and gratefully applaud all my limbs and organs that are still working. In that way, the things I can be grateful for increase every day. "My cup overflows" (Ps 23:5).

Daily it becomes clearer to me: gratitude is a celebration of love. Just as love is the lived yes of joyful mutual belonging, gratitude celebrates life with a joyful yes at every knot of the great network in which everything is connected. As we live this yes with more conviction, love ripens in and around us in ever greater summer. I now see that as my main task, since "man dies not from death, but by overripe love."[9]

DIALOGUE

JK: Brother David, you began your description of the most recent decade of your life by relating an encounter you had with a gorilla in a zoo. That led you to reflect on the idea that we are essentially all living in a double realm: the intellectual and the emotional, the body and the soul, the profane and the holy, time and infinity. The question is how are these double realms connected, or rather how can you, yourself, manage to exist in these double realms without suffering from a kind of split personality or split soul?

DSR: We see these kinds of antitheses everywhere, and the important insight is that while we can distinguish between them, we must never separate them. They are opposites, but they are closely connected and interdependent. They do not polarize life, they are poles of an indivisible oneness. At a significant moment in one of his poems, Clemens Brentano points to the poles of living a life fully: "O star and flower, spirit and garment, love, suffering and time and eternity."[10] Rilke coined the beautiful phrase "double realm"[11] to describe this relationship.

JK: So, the practice consists of repeatedly putting oneself into or reimmersing oneself in what one might call this ontological realm, if I understand you correctly? That reminds me of the ontological difference between Being and beings.

DSR: We can avoid polarization by looking at one pole and already seeing the other pole within it. So, for example, I look at time and in that time experience eternity, that very Now that extends beyond time. Or I look at suffering and see in it the earthly face of love. I look at a star and see the flower in it, or I look at the flower and see the star in it. The entire cosmos is a double realm.

JK: You write that you are aware of oneness only if you live in the Now, in the moment, in the double realm of time and eternity. When you hang on to the past or get entangled in fantasies of the future, oneness becomes constraining and oppressive. Then you become aware of the shortness of life. That in turn can spark fear, fear of death. What is the thing that makes you anxious?

DSR: There are two things that make me personally anxious when I think of death. First, there is the fact that we do not know what awaits us in death. We simply do not know. We are walking toward something that is not only unknown to us, but completely and utterly unimaginable. How can a caterpillar in a cocoon imagine what it is like to flutter from flower to flower as a butterfly? We too are walking toward something completely new. But things that are knew and unknown make us anxious. Second, we know that death is often connected to illness, suffering, and pain. That alone is enough to make me anxious when I picture it. Added to that, there is the prospect that today, sooner or later, one turns into nothing more than a case or a number in a hospital. This depersonalization makes me anxious as well. But quite apart from aging and dying, life is always scaring us in some way or another. What we need is courage.

I Am Because of You

JK: And what gives you courage, in this context?

DSR: Simply put: trust in life. If my life's path narrows and I become anxious, my trust in life becomes essential. Fear resists the anxiety and gets stuck in it. But trust lets itself be propelled forward and upward; it commits itself to the upward currents of life, like swimming.

JK: You say that you do not want to speak of a life after death. Is there really that much room for misunderstanding?

DSR: Unfortunately, the language can easily be misunderstood, because it sounds as though I mean that with death, everything stops. That is not at all what I want to say. What I mean is that with death, my time has run out, and when there is no more time, the word *after* means very little. I die when my time has run out, so how can I talk about something *after*? Time ends with death. My life ends on the level of time and space—I do not want to trivialize or idealize that. I want to confront it honestly: in my death, my space-time ends. But that does not mean that everything is over. Not at all! Even in the midst of time and space—in experiencing the Now—I experience a dimension that extends beyond time and space, and that is not defeated by death.

Admittedly, I cannot avoid one difficulty: a person could say, "I have experience only through my senses, which are in time and space; I can think only with my brain, but when my brain turns to dust, what then?" In response, I can only say that here and now my senses and my thinking bring me to the border of something that extends beyond space and time, is unbounded by space and time. And I belong to this dimension of my being—the Lasting—as much as I belong to time and space. That is exactly the double realm in which I live. This experience gives me trust and faith in something lasting, even when my bodily reality ends. Even now, I can touch a lasting reality. In the Now, I approach the Lasting. I need to be open to that, and must feel my way into the

Now and make a home for myself there. This consciousness can easily get lost in the gears of time.

JK: No small number of Christians have trouble with the problem of a corporeal resurrection, because they think of it primarily as the resurrection of a body. But we can see that the body disintegrates, reenters the big cycle of nature. That is the most obvious thing and can be proved.

But Christianity nevertheless claims a corporeal resurrection. What might that mean?

DSR: Before we talk about that, it is important to know what we even mean when we say "resurrection." Most people think of it very literally as a re-surrection, standing up again, coming back from something that has died and fallen apart. But a true understanding of resurrection does not include any return. Resurrection does not go back to time and space but forward into the Great Mystery. C. S. Lewis's novel *The Great Divorce* describes this movement "forward" beautifully.[12] The blessed in heaven ride toward an eternal sunrise and urge one another onward. This idea has deep roots in the Christian tradition. It goes back—as C. S. Lewis may have been aware—to the Cappadocian Fathers, who thought of a lived resurrection as a dynamic journey of discovery into the Mystery of God.[13] Resurrection means being brought into the Mystery. This is the light in which we must see resurrection of the flesh. It is a reality with which we are in touch even now. Our entire life consists of engaging, amid time and space, with the Great Mystery that extends beyond time and space. Even now, any experience in the double realm partakes of both these aspects. So, when time and space fall away, the experiences that I have had are not obliterated. Our memory, the fact that we can remember anything, shows us that much.

JK: But memory is a phenomenon of time.

I Am Because of You

DSR: Memory is a phenomenon *in* time, but it is a very reduction-ist idea that memory is *only* in time. Yes, there are things such as neural constellations or engrams, records of some kind that are then accessed; there is something to that. But the essential part of memory is different. Memory is not just the recall of past things, it is something that has entered deep into us and is not only a part of my personal interior but of the whole interior world. Rilke turns that into the poetic idea that we are the "bees of the invisible." Our entire lives consist of harvesting every moment, every experience into the "great golden honeycomb" of the interior world. Nothing can ever be lost there. What I have stored there is my unique contribution. We are so different that there have probably never been two people who have looked at, for example, a rose and seen the same thing. With my unique sensibility, I enrich the interior world. I enrich it over the course of my entire life, not just in pleasant experiences, but with all my suffering as well. Everything has worth and constancy. Nothing is lost.

JK: We hope that suffering, too, will be transformed. So, let me ask again in a different way. Is transience transformed as well?

DSR: It is transformed even now. Now or never. The mystic poet, Kabir, asks, "If you as a living being do not break your chains, shall spirits do so when you are dead?" What he means is that eternal blessedness, simply because one is being eaten by worms, is wishful thinking. What you find now you will have found then, what you neglect now you will have neglected then. You must receive and embrace the Great Guest even now.

JK: I need to dig a little deeper there. If I am understanding you correctly, intransience means being removed from the temporal stream of transience. In some sense, we cannot think of it any other way, being bodily creatures. It is obvious that the body changes even during our lifetime. But I am thinking of our form—we are always form and thus recognizable. If I am lucky enough, Brother David, I would like to meet you again in heaven at the "honeycomb"—and be able to recognize you.

DSR: Even now, it is the case that after twenty years, we have no difficulty in recognizing an old acquaintance, and yet no cell in his body remains the same. What we recognize is the form. And "form of the body" is the definition of the *soul*.

JK: *Anima forma corporis est*, as scholastic theologians have said. "Soul is the form of the body."[14]

DSR: It is what makes this body this body—and not just body, but what makes this person this unique person.

JK: The soul is that aliveness.

DSR: In the double realm, we all have double aliveness: in time and space and in the Great Self that extends beyond time and space.

JK: Brother David, I cannot help noticing how intensely your life's path is accompanied by art: its beginnings in visual arts, but also by music and especially by literature and poetry. Clearly, you admire Rilke, Eichendorff, Morgenstern, Trakl, Celan, and Stifter. In Germany, the North American poets—David White, T. S. Eliot, E. E. Cummings—are less well-known. The last of these has a special significance for you.[15]

DSR: Cummings's poetry has grown very dear to me and is very close to my heart. The quote of his that is most important to me is "I am through you so I." It is from a love poem that simultaneously has overtones of a prayer, just like Rilke's "Extinguish my eyes" was a love poem and was then inserted into the *Book of Hours* as a prayer.[16] Our deepest and most alive relationships in life always resonate with the Great Mystery. I could not express my own lifelong relationship with the Divine Mystery any more fittingly than in the sentence "I am through you so I." What makes us a person is the richness and depth of our relationships, and we constantly grow through each new encounter. And our relationship with the eternal You resonates in each of our human encounters, too—I am *because of* you. Ferdinand Ebner and Martin Buber each in their own way demonstrated what this "I am through you so I" means: beyond each human You, we are in relation to a mysterious primeval You, mysterious in the sense that it lies hidden in the Mystery and the Mystery, itself, becomes You to us. The only reason we can say "I" at all is that we are in relation to the Mystery, so I really am because of You.

I remember how in my early years as a monk, I would wander over the hills around the monastery, simply praying the word *You*, over and over. The same thing is said of a Hasidic teacher, that he prayed, "You, you, you!" Is that not prayer enough?

JK: It reminds one of the Prayer of the Heart.

DSR: Yes, a great deal. The Prayer of the Heart is also a prayer to the You, in the end. The older I become, the more important this "I am through you so I" becomes for me. When our I passes out of space and time, our relationship with the primeval You remains. That was and is the fundamental First from which everything comes, and it will be the Last that remains. And for me, this sentence of "I am through you so I" belongs in a context with Rilke's stanza:

> When I go toward you
> it is with my whole life.
> [For who am I and who are you
> if we do not understand each other?][17]

Taken together, these two poetic insights give me more direction in my life than all philosophical and theological explications.

JK: Because they come closest to the essence of the phenomenon, one could say?

DSR: Yes, one can put it like that.

JK: Brother David, I have no idea yet what it feels like to be ninety years old, and I am sure that there is a great deal that I am facing in that. But I am not the only one who admires how awake, curious, alive you still are at your age. What occupies, drives, moves you today in this possibly last full decade of your life?

DSR: More and more clearly, my great task has crystallized as living in the Now and continuing to practice that. I see that as my main task and simultaneously as a great gift, being able to practice that for so many long decades. Perhaps our life is only prolonged because we have not yet learned to fully live in the Now.

JK: What gives you joy today—what still fills you with wonder and opens wide your heart?

DSR: To answer that question, I would need to list everything I encounter over the course of the day. Everything fills me with wonder, more than ever. It starts when I open my eyes in the morning: the fact that I am given one more day, is that not a great surprise?

JK: I am still here...

DSR: Aha! I am still around! Everything, everything becomes more worthy of wonder.

JK: More worthy of wonder, the older you become—how? After all, you could also say, "I am inured, I've seen this before."

DSR: As Augustine says, "All is given, all is grace, all is gift."

JK: Brother David, thank you for speaking with me.

DSR: I thank you for your questions.

NOTES

1. BECOMING HUMAN

1. I started walking at nine months, so I may have been three years old at the time of this memory.

2. My father had inherited the *Café Siller* in the *Schönbrunner Allee* from his uncle Franz Siller. The "Maria Theresa Palace" (*Maria Theresien Schlössl*) of the *Café Meierei Siller*, also called the "Marienvilla," was a handsome building with plasterwork ceilings, baroque fireplaces, and parquet flooring in star patterns.

3. Hans, born December 14, 1928, and Max, born thirteen months later on January 17, 1930.

4. Supposedly, *detta* is a Czech term of endearment meaning "auntie"—but in our case, it came from our early attempts to say *Schwester*, the German short form of "children's nurse." We loved our Detta—Elfriede Gödel. She came when I was approximately three years old and stayed with us over more than twenty years, far into our adulthood.

5. IMI was a brand of detergent introduced by the Henkel company in 1929.

6. This dream became fundamental in that the image of merging with Christ fits as well with all subsequent phases of my becoming fully human. The dream did not, however, produce in me any feelings of awe or reverence. In fact, it was not emotional

at all. Instead, I would say that it sparked an insight in me that was far beyond my comprehension at the time but stayed in my memory as significant for perhaps that very reason.

7. Molybdomancy became a common New Year tradition in the Nordic countries and Germany, Switzerland, and Austria. Classically, tin is melted on a stove and poured into a bucket of cold water. The resulting shape is either directly interpreted as an omen for the future, or it is rotated in candlelight to create shadows, whose shapes are then interpreted.

8 Plato, *Theaetetus*, trans. Benjamin Jowett (Teddington: Echo Library, 2006), 155d: "This feeling of wonder shows that you are a philosopher, since wonder is the only beginning of philosophy."

9. Theodor Haecker (1879–1945) was a German writer, cultural critic, and translator. He was among Catholic existentialism's most eloquent defenders and one of the most radical cultural critics of the Weimar Republic and the Third Reich.

10. Pius Parsch (1884–1954) was an Austrian Catholic priest whose writings contributed significantly to the liturgical movement. He was also highly interested in reevaluating the Bible with an eye to liturgical practice. As military curate on the Easter Front of the First World War, he encountered the liturgy of Orthodox Christian churches and decided to make the Bible a book for the people and liturgy comprehensible to all. After his return to Klosterneuburg Abbey, he held Scripture courses for the novices. From 1922 onward, he celebrated community masses in which large parts of the Mass would be sung in German (the local language; these masses are commonly known as the *Betsingmesse*, or *Deutsche Singmesse*)—with the goal of encouraging more active participation by those hearing the Mass, as well as a return to early Christian service practices. His services are considered the origins of the liturgical movement in Austria.

2. BECOMING CHRISTLIKE

1. The Catholic youth movement *Bund Neuland* (Newland Union) was founded in 1921 as an offshoot of the *Christlich-deutscher Studentenbund*, or "Christian German Student Union." After the annexation of Austria in 1938, the *Bund* dissolved itself, but was reestablished in 1948. In 1927, Anna Ehm and a group of young teachers from the *Bund Neuland* founded the *Neuland-schule* (Newland School) in Grinzing, which was reopened in 1946; a new *Neulandschule* on the *Laaer Berg* followed in 1947. The pedagogical concept of the schools was based on holistic education in teaching and recreation, unhurried communication of knowledge, encouragement of community life, purposeful awakening of creative capacities, and Christian values as an orientation in life.

2. From Werner Bergengruen's "Poeta creator":

> Everything I created with you in mind,
> For your well-being;
> Then willingly accept the world,
> and with wakeful courage.
> Since as love created it
> even unto the poorest seedling—
> There is nothing that may frighten you,
> And you are at home.

3. The text of the song translates to "Thoughts are free / who may guess what they are? / They fly past / like shadows in the night. / No person can know them, / no hunter can shoot them. / The fact remains: / thoughts are free."

4. Ps 51:12: "*Redde mihi laetitiam salutaris tui, et spiritum principali confirma me*—Restore to me the joy of your salvation, and sustain in me a willing spirit."

5. Ferdinand Ebner (1882–1931) was an elementary school teacher in Gablitz near Vienna and a personal-dialogical philosopher who, together with Martin Buber, is considered one of the most

significant dialogical thinkers. His most important work is *The Word and its Spiritual Realities: Pneumatological Fragments* (1921).

6. *Gröfaz* was a nickname mockingly given to Adolf Hitler after the defeat of the German troops at Stalingrad in 1943. It is the abbreviation of the (ironic) German words for "greatest commander of all time," *größter Feldherr aller Zeiten*.

7. Reinhold Schneider (1903–58) was a German writer. His last book was *Winter in Vienna* (1957/58).

8. Friedrich Heer (1916–83) was a cultural historian, writer, and editor. The most thematically relevant of his many works is perhaps *Der Glaube des Adolf Hitler. Anatomie einer politischen Religiosität* (*The Faith of Adolf Hitler: Anatomy of a Political Religiousness*) (Vienna, 1968).

9. Adolf Hitler, *My Struggle*, trans. unknown (London: Hurst and Blackett, 1938).

10. Eric Voegelin (1901–85) was a German-American political scientist and philosopher. The fifth volume of his *Collected Works* (St. Louis: University of Missouri Press, 1999) contains *The Political Religions* as well as *The New Science of Politics* and *Science, Politics, and Gnosticism*.

11. *sub specie boni* (lat.): under the sight of the good, that is, from the point of view of goodness.

12. Vienna's tram line 38 ends at *Am Schottenring* station (informally known as "Jonas-Reindl") near the University of Vienna.

13. Bruno Brehm (1892–1974), who wrote under the pen name of Bruno Clemens, was an Austrian author. He was a member of the national socialist Bamberg Poets' Circle and publisher of the periodical *Der getreue Eckart* from 1938 to 1942.

14. In "Mankind" (*Menschheit*, trans. James Reidel, *Mudlark* 53 [2014]), Austrian poet Georg Trakl (1887–1914) writes,

> Mankind marched up before fiery jaws,
> A drumroll, the gloomy soldiers' foreheads,
> Footsteps through a bloody fog; black iron rings,

Desperation, night in sorrowful minds:
Here Eve's shadow, a manhunt and red coin.
Clouds, the light is breaking through, the Last Supper.
A gentle silence dwells in bread and wine.
And those gathered here are twelve in number.
Nights they moan asleep beneath olive boughs;
Saint Thomas dips his hand in the wound's mark.

15. Ernst Wiechert (1887–1950) was among the most widely read German writers of the "Inner Emigration" under National Socialism.

16. Georg Thurmair (1909–84) was a German writer, poet, journalist, and documentary filmmaker. He authored approximately three hundred German-language hymns.

17. Theodor Innitzer (1875–1955) was the archbishop of Vienna, as well as a professor of New Testament studies and sometime social minister under Engelbert Dollfuß's Austro-fascist government.

3. DECISION

1. Father Heinrich Maier (1908–45) was an Austrian Roman Catholic priest, pedagogue, and philosopher. He fought in the resistance against Hitler.

2. 1 Kgs 3:16–28: Later, two women who were prostitutes came to the king and stood before him. The one woman said, "Please, my lord, this woman and I live in the same house; and I gave birth while she was in the house. Then on the third day after I gave birth, this woman also gave birth. We were together; there was no one else with us in the house, only the two of us were in the house. Then this woman's son died in the night, because she lay on him. She got up in the middle of the night and took my son from beside me while your servant slept. She laid him at her breast, and laid her dead son at my breast. When I rose in

the morning to nurse my son, I saw that he was dead; but when I looked at him closely in the morning, clearly it was not the son I had borne." But the other woman said, "No, the living son is mine, and the dead son is yours." The first said, "No, the dead son is yours, and the living son is mine." So they argued before the king.

Then the king said, "The one says, 'This is my son that is alive, and your son is dead'; while the other says, 'Not so! Your son is dead, and my son is the living one.'" So the king said, "Bring me a sword," and they brought a sword before the king. The king said, "Divide the living boy in two; then give half to the one, and half to the other." But the woman whose son was alive said to the king—because compassion for her son burned within her—"Please, my lord, give her the living boy; certainly do not kill him!" The other said, "It shall be neither mine nor yours; divide it." Then the king responded: "Give the first woman the living boy; do not kill him. She is his mother." All Israel heard of the judgment that the king had rendered; and they stood in awe of the king, because they perceived that the wisdom of God was in him, to execute justice.

3. *Der goldene Wagen* (The Golden Wagon) (1947–49). The first issue of the first volume is published Easter 1947. Characterized by attractive design and pictures, the periodical continues to appear monthly, in DIN A4 format, until the third volume, which is somewhat larger.

4. *Sterz* refers to a way of preparing simple dishes with small chunks of buckwheat flour (*Heidensterz*), cornmeal (*Türkensterz*), rye flour (*Brennsterz*), semolina (*Grießsterz*), potatoes (*Erdäpfelsterz*), or beans (*Bohnensterz*). *Sterz* was a typical "poor people's food," and today, farmers and field workers in Carinthia (*Kärnten*) and Styria (*Steiermark*) still frequently eat *Sterz* with bacon fat and cracklings as a hearty breakfast.

5. The Monastery community of Mount Saviour was founded in 1950/52 by Fathers Damasus Winzen from Maria Laach, Gregory Bornstedt, and Placid Cormey, the latter two from Portsmouth Priory, Rhode Island.

6. Wilhelm Koppers, SVD (1886–1961), was a German Catholic priest and ethnographer, as well as a Steyler missionary and early member of the "Vienna *Kulturkreis* School" in cultural anthropology. He was considered a vehement critic and opponent of National Socialist race theory.

7. Wilhelm Schmidt, SVD (1868–1954), was a Roman Catholic priest, linguist, and ethnographer. He founded the "Vienna *Kulturkreis* School," which attempted to develop a universal history of culture; Schmidt is today considered one of the early twentieth century's most significant comparative linguists.

8. Hubert Rohracher (1903–72) was an Austrian psychologist, philosopher, and jurist. His arguably most famous work, *Persönlichkeit und Schicksal* (Personality and Fate), was published in Vienna in 1926.

9. Walter Schücker, OCist (1913–77), was confessor, counselor, and leader of spiritual exercises at the Cistercian Abbey of *Heiligenkreuz*. In 1951, he and Abbot Karl Braunstorfer founded the prayer community "Friends of the Holy Cross," which today counts eighteen hundred members. They subsequently founded the *Heiligenkreuz* Oblate community in 1972.

10. Paul Claudel (1868–1955) was a French writer, poet, and diplomat.

4. BECOMING A MONK

1. German poet Rainer Maria Rilke (1875–1926) writes the following in his *Sonnets to Orpheus* I,7, in *The Poetry of Rilke*, trans. Edward Snow (New York: North Point, 2009), 363:

> Praising, that's it! One appointed to praise
> he came forth like ore out of the stone's
> silence. His heart, O ephemeral winepress
> for a vintage eternal to man.

I Am Because of You

Never does his voice die or turn to dust
when the divine moment seizes him.
All becomes vineyard, all becomes grape,
ripened in his sentient South.

Not mold in the vaults of kings
nor any shadow falling from the gods
can give his songs the lie.

He is one of the messengers who stay,
holding far into the doors of the dead
bowls heaped with fruit to be praised.

2. John Henry Newman (1801–90), *The Mission of the Benedictine Order*.

3. See Gen 2:19: So out of the ground the LORD God formed every animal of the field and every bird of the air, and brought them to the man to see what he would call them; and whatever the man called every living creature, that was its name.

4. The Abbaye Saint-Pierre de Solesmes is a Benedictine monastery in Solesmes in the French *département* of Sarthe.

5. Rainer Maria Rilke, "Es winkt zu Fühlung fast aus allen Dingen," trans. David Young, *Cortland Review* (Summer 2013).

6. Rainer Maria Rilke, *Sonnets to Orpheus* I,9. in *Duino Elegies & the Sonnets to Orpheus*, trans. Stephen Mitchell (New York: Vintage, 2009), 99.

7. Rainer Maria Rilke, Duino Elegies, I, Ninth Elegy, in *Duino Elegies & the Sonnets to Orpheus*, 57.

8. T. S. Eliot, "Burnt Norton," from *Four Quartets*, in *Collected Poems 1909–1962* (New York: Harcourt Brace & Company, 1991), 180.

9. Raimon Panikkar (1918–2010) was a Roman Catholic priest from Catalonia, Spain. He was a significant proponent of interfaith dialogue and published numerous works on the subject, including *The Trinity and the Religious Experience of Man* and *The Silence of God, the Answer of the Buddha*.

10. Joseph Gredt, OSB (1863–1940), from Luxembourg was a Benedictine monk and philosophy professor in Rome.

11. Evagrius Ponticus (345–399) was an Egyptian monk and theologian who lived in the Nitrian desert with other desert fathers. He originated the "eight patterns of evil," which were then taken up and developed by John Cassian and survive today as the doctrine of the Seven Deadly Sins.

12. The *Apophthegmata Patrum* is a collection of sayings (*apophthegmata*) and stories attributed to the desert fathers of the fourth and fifth centuries AD. The sayings of Abba Poemen, Abba Macarius of Egypt, and Anthony the Great are among the more well-known. The *apophthegmata* are similar to the koans of Zen Buddhism.

13. Rabbi Samson ben Raphael Hirsch (1808–88) was one of nineteenth-century Germany's leading proponents of Orthodox Judaism and founder of neo-Orthodoxy.

14. Abraham Joshua Heschel (1907–72) was a rabbi, writer, and Jewish religious philosopher of Polish descent. Exiled to the United States, he was active in the civil rights movement. His writing—such as *Man's Quest for God* (New York: Scribner, 1954)—and engagement were officially honored by Pope Paul VI, among others.

15. Rainer Maria Rilke, "Archaic Torso of Apollo", in *The Poetry of Rilke*, ed. and trans. Edward Snow (New York: North Point Press, 2009), 223.

16. Friedrich Nietzsche, *Beyond Good and Evil: Prelude to a Philosophy of the Future*, trans. Judith Norman. ed. Judith Norman and Peter Horstmann (Cambridge: Cambridge University Press, 2002), 4.

17. Friedrich Nietzsche, *The Gay Science: With a Prelude in Rhymes and an Appendix of Songs*, trans. Walter Kaufmann (New York: Vintage Books, 1974), 181.

18. Negative theology attempts to marry religious faith with the philosophy of reason and to explain religious faith using

philosophical tools. It denies the possibility of objective knowledge or proof of God. Characteristics, names, or definitions of the Divine are likewise dismissed as insufficient to describe the distinction of the Divine Mystery. One of negative theology's most well-known proponents is the medieval theologian and philosopher Meister Eckhart.

5. INTERFAITH DIALOGUE

1. Gustav Mensching (1901–78) was a scholar of comparative religion whose academic contributions play an important role in interfaith dialogue even today. Mensching was partly responsible for the separation of religious studies from theology and the establishment of the former as an independent discipline of inquiry. Mensching saw religion as "the experiential encounter with the Holy, and responsive action by persons motivated by the Holy" (Stuttgart: Curt E. Schwab, 1959, 18–19; excerpt translated by Peter Dahm Robertson).

2. Thich Nhat Hanh (born 1926) is a Vietnamese Buddhist monk, poet, author, and founder of study centers.

3. David Steindl-Rast, *Deeper Than Words: Living the Apostles' Creed* (New York: Doubleday Religion, 2010).

4. The Global Ethic is the formulation of a fundamental stock of ethical norms and values that can be derived from religious, cultural, and even philosophical traditions throughout human history. The "Global Ethics Project" is an attempt to describe similarities of the world's religions and to develop out of these fundamental norms a shared Ethic, a brief set of rules that can be accepted by all. The project was initiated by theologian Hans Küng.

5. Gustav Mensching refers to this Mystery as "the Holy," and Rudolf Otto has shown that when we encounter the Holy, we are fascinated and thrilled—that is to say, reverent.

6. *Stabilitas loci* (Latin for "fixedness of place") refers to a nun's or monk's connection to a specific monastery.

7. This second line of the Lutheran hymn "*O Lamm Gottes unschuldig*" (O Lamb of God so blameless), well-known throughout German churches, translates to "You have borne all sin / Else we would have to despair."

8. Joseph von Eichendorff (1788–1857) was one of German Romanticism's most significant poets and lyricists. The quoted poem is an excerpt from "*Der Umkehrende*" (Turning Back), translated by Peter Dahm Robertson.

6. A HERMIT'S LIFE

1. In the style of Theophane the Monk, in *Tales of a Magic Monastery* (New York: The Crossroad Publishing Company, 1981).

2. Rainer Maria Rilke, *The Selected Poetry of Rainer Maria Rilke*, trans. Stephen Mitchel (New York: Vintage Books, 1982), 143.

3. Bear Island lies off the coast of Maine and is one of the five Cranberry Isles.

4. Rilke, *Sonnets to Orpheus*, II,23, in *Duino Elegies & the Sonnets to Orpheus*, trans. Stephen Mitchell (New York: Vintage, 2009).

5. Kathleen Jessie Raine, CBE, (1908–2003) was a British poet, academic, and literary critic. Her writing focused particularly on the works of William Blake, W. B. Yeats, and Thomas Taylor. Founder of the Temenos Academy, she was also highly interested in all forms of spirituality.

6. "Alone with the Alone," or with the All-One. It is one of my favorite phrases used by John Henry Cardinal Newman, referring to his relationship with God as a face-to-face encounter that none should come between. As a young and lonely man at Oriel College, he was once greeted on a solitary stroll by Edward Copleston, who, with a gentlemanly bow, said, "*Numquam minus solus quam cum solus!*" (Never less alone than when alone!). Solitude, many saints

have learned, is where one best finds God, and solitude cannot be had without silence.

7. Scetis refers to the Wadi El-Natrun, a desert valley in Egypt. The name *Scetis* comes from the Ancient Egyptian *Sekhet-hemat*, meaning "salt field." The Wadi remains a site of hermitages and monasteries.

8. Henry David Thoreau (1817–62) was an American philosopher and author. He is best known for his book *Walden; Or, Life in the Woods* and his essay "Civil Disobedience."

7. ENCOUNTERS IN TRAVEL

1. The *Kohte* was a type of tent that originated in (autonomous) German youth movements. It was developed around 1930 by Eberhard Koebel, based on a tent design of the Finnish Saami people (near Inari lake).

2. The Puszta is the large steppe region leading from eastern Austria and Hungary all the way to Mongolia. It is probable that Austrian youth movements encountered these kinds of long-handled spoons on visits to this region, as trips to Hungary, Romania, and other parts of Eastern Europe were popular.

3. Cardinal Pio Taofinu'u, SM (1923–2006), was the archbishop of Samoa-Apia.

4. For the definition and description of a *marae*, see https://en.wikipedia.org/wiki/Marae.

5. The meaning of *Puja* approximates to "honoring" or "doing honor." As a ritual, which should ideally be practiced daily, it is one of the primary parts of everyday religious practice in both Hinduism and Buddhism.

6. Bede Griffiths (1906–93) was a British Benedictine monk and one of the twentieth century's best known mystics. From 1968

onward, he led the Shantivanam ashram and monastery. He is particularly known for his religious dialogue with Hinduism.

7. Rainer Maria Rilke, *Rilke's Book of Hours: Love Poems to God*, trans. Anita Barrows and Joanna Macy (New York: Riverhead Books, 1996), 84.

8. CONTEMPLATION AND REVOLUTION

1. *Sangha* is the community of lay faithful and ordained clergy who mutually support one another in following the Buddha and the Dharma. Regardless of the exact definition, all traditions view *sangha* as one of the Buddhism's "Three Jewels" or "Three Treasures."

2. See http://www.gratefulness.org, http://viviragradecidos.org, and others.

3. Dorothy Day (1897–1980) was an American Christian Socialist and journalist. Until 1927, she was a radical communist; after her conversion to Catholicism in 1928, she advocated a Christian anarchism. Together with Peter Maurin, she founded the Catholic Worker Movement and was imprisoned several times because, as both a committed suffragist and pacifist, she could not reconcile her conscience and faith to contemporary political developments. In 2000, Pope John Paul II granted the New York Archdiocese permission to open her cause for canonization.

4. Friedrich Hölderlin (1770–1843), from "An Zimmern"; excerpt translated by Peter Dahm Robertson.

5. Pope Francis, *Evangelii Gaudium* (The Joy of the Gospel), no. 53.

6. See www.gratefulness.org.

9. DOUBLE REALM

1. Rainer Maria Rilke, *Sonnets to Orpheus* I,9, in *The Poetry of Rilke*, trans. Edward Snow (New York: North Point, 2009), 367.

2. T. S. Eliot, "Little Gidding," from *Four Quartets*, in *Collected Poems 1909–1962* (New York: Harcourt Brace & Company, 1991), 204.

3. Rainer Maria Rilke, *Rilke's Book of Hours: Love Poems to God*, trans. Anita Barrows and Joanna Macy (New York: Riverhead Books, 1996), 69.

4. Dupuytren's contracture is a thickening and shortening of the connective tissues (fascia) of the palm, most commonly observed around Haithabu, the Viking capital.

5. From the poem "Es ist doch alles nur aus Liebe gut" by German poet and literary critic Will Vesper (1882–1962). Excerpt translated by Peter Dahm Robertson.

6. T. S. Eliot, "The Dry Salvages," from *Four Quartets* in *Collected Poems 1909–1962*, 199.

7. Rainer Maria Rilke: "Nous sommes les abeilles de l'Univers. Nous butinons éperdument le miel du visible, pour l'accumuler dans la grande ruche d'or de l'Invisible." Letter to W. von Hulewicz.

8. W. B. Yeats, "Sailing to Byzantium," accessed March 21, 2017, https://www.poetryfoundation.org/poems-and-poets/poems/detail/43291.

9. P. Otto Mauer, summarizing Thornton Wilder's novel *The Bridge of San Luis Rey*.

10. Excerpt from Clemens Brentano's (1778–1842) poem "Was reif in diesen Zeilen steht" (What stands in these lines, ripe), translated by Peter Dahm Robertson.

11. *Sonnets to Orpheus* I, 9.

12. Clive Staples Lewis (1898–1963) was an Irish writer and literary scholar. In addition to his scholarship and criticism, he also published many works of Christian apologia (e.g., *Mere*

Christianity and *The Abolition of Man*) and novels such as *The Great Divorce* and *The Chronicles of Narnia*.

13. Cappadocia is a region in Asia Minor. In the fourth century AD, it was home to many significant figures in early Christianity. Three of these—Basil the Great, Gregory of Nyssa, and Gregory of Nazianzus—are today known as the Cappadocian Fathers. They were early advocates of a trinitarian theory of God as God-Father, God-Son, and God-Holy Spirit.

14. The definition is taken from Thomas Aquinas.

15. Edward Estlin Cummings (1894–1962) was an American poet and writer.

16. "Extinguish My Eyes, I'll Go on Seeing You." Rainer Maria Rilke, *Rilke's Book of Hours: Love Poems to God*, 111–12.

17. "Only in Our Doing Can We Grasp You," from Rainer Maria Rilke, *Rilke's Book of Hours: Love Poems to God*, 84; last two lines appended to incomplete translation.

ABOUT THE INTERVIEWER

Johannes Kaup studied Philosophy and Catholic Theology in Vienna and is a trained psychotherapist in the analysis of life. He has been active in the field of youth social work and as a religious lecturer. Since 1990, he has been working at the ORF, where he has conceived and moderated programs in religion, science, and education.

He has received numerous awards as a journalist, among others with the "Radiopreis de Erwachsenenbildung," the "Austrian Climate Protection Prize," the "Seniors' Rose," and the "Dr. Karl Renner Prize for Literature" in the Radio category.

Johannes Kaup has been a moderator at international congresses and has published five books.